PRAISE FOR BODY BEAUTIFUL

"Suzzi has created a much needed guide for coming back to self and honouring the body we've neglected for far too long."

— Jordanna Levin, Bestselling Author of *Higher Love and Make It Happen*

"In a world of omni-present impossibly perfect body-beautiful images, this book is a must-read for every woman. Do yourself a favour and read this, then share it with your girlfriends and daughters."

— Sally O'Neil, The Fit Foodie @thefitfoodieblog

"Everyone who reads *Body Beautiful* will take something meaningful and significant away with them. Regardless of age, job title or how society has left you viewing yourself (and others), it is the soul glow-up read you've been looking for."

— Lee Sutherland, Director of frankie+jet and Founder of Little Wildling Co organic teas

"What a gift to the world this book is. The beautiful expansion I experienced in my chest while reading the pages is a true indication of its high vibrational content, that will be absorbed as medicine for every reader that is lucky enough to come across these pages. It's everything I have ever learnt in the world of energy and rewiring patterns in one neat little bundle.
All we need is consciousness and courage, no truer words spoken."

— Tash White, founder of The Soul Intuitive

"*Body Beautiful* is a masterpiece that appealed to both my masculine logical brain that needs to understand how things work in order to transcend them, and my feminine emotional brain that just desires to be heard and understood. The way the book was written made me feel like Suzzi herself was reaching out her hand, taking mine, and saying to me warmly 'I know how it feels, I see you, and let me walk beside you while you soften and learn how to do life differently'. *Body Beautiful* creates a loving check in with ourselves to bring awareness to the areas of our life we have allowed weeds to grow in, and empowers us with tools and wisdom to create a new way of being.
A true and loving Bestie in book form."

— Tamara Northam

BODY
BEAUTIFUL

Your Guide to Making Peace with Your Body
and Letting Yourself Bloom

SUZZI HARTERY

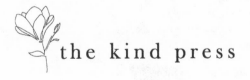

the kind press

Illustrations by Suzzi Hartery
Cover design: Mila Graphic Artist
Internal design: Nicola Matthews, Nikki Jane Design
Edited by Ally McManus

Cataloguing-in-Publication
entry is available from the
National Library Australia.

NATIONAL
LIBRARY
OF AUSTRALIA

ISBN: 978-0-6488706-9-2
ISBN: 978-0-6450113-5-7 (ebook)

To all the women who were told or whom ever think
their body isn't beautiful
~ now is the time to believe it is, and always has been!

'What if you started to appreciate yourself, just a little more each day … imagine how different you would feel in a week, a month, a year? This is my big-hearted wish for you!'
~ Suzzi Hartery

CONTENTS

PART B
The Expedition – Letting Your Beauty Bloom

'Every flower is a soul blossoming in nature.'
~ Gerard De Nerval

INTRODUCTION

Have you ever wondered why flowers fill us with such delight and inspiration? The colours can uplift the saddest of hearts and restore our faith in the beauty of this world. The scent can take us to places of peace and remind us of times when we felt happy and free. Yet, there is much more to the story than the blossom that captures our immediate attention. The flower exists for us to enjoy because it has undertaken its own growth journey. It only exists and brings us joy because the seed was planted in the right conditions and was nurtured through its path of growth. The flower you see is the result of an arduous expedition—from seed to flower. The flower you see that is blooming is the outcome of a dedicated process of *becoming*.

Like the Earth, the trees and the flowers, each of us is part of the natural world that surrounds us. The same basic rules of survival govern our existence. Our bodies depend on the same fundamental needs, being shelter, food and water. But as humans, there is one significant difference. While the weather and predators batter the flora of this Earth, one of the greatest battles we face through this life is our psyche. When we unconsciously buy into the expectations of others, we can be tossed around by their whims and left feeling weather-beaten. Our own limiting beliefs, thoughts and feelings are the most significant barriers to our ability to thrive.

Throughout each day, we face so many questions about our direction, purpose and actions. In every moment we juggle the options of pursuing our dreams and what feels right in our hearts or following the tribe. All of these conflicting expectations can feel so exhausting. Some days, they are almost debilitating, leaving an overwhelming feeling of despair or being stuck. Living with these conundrums, this multitude of choices takes its toll on your mind, body and spirit.

But there is some good news. There is a way you can break free from being tossed around by your expectations and the opinions of others. There is a way that you can decide which path to take with clarity, courage and peace. You see, already within you, you have the power to move through each day working with your body, mind and spirit, rather than against them. You already have the wisdom within you to bring acceptance, kindness, and love to yourself every day. You have the power within you to give the care and compassion to yourself that you may show to others so naturally and readily. You have the innate ability to make peace with your body and to love being you. Let yourself bloom!

But what does this take?

It takes two things: consciousness and courage.

Consciousness

First, consciousness is required to see and understand the forces that are pushing and pulling us. While there are many rules for how we live that are written and enforced through formal authorities, there are also endless influences upon us that are unconscious. These can take the form of events and role models from our past, which still show up in our lives today and potentially haunt our thoughts and feelings. Perhaps there was unspoken favouritism in your family to a member who was deemed more physically beautiful than you. Maybe there was an overt and painful comparison by those you relied on for love and support. This past hurt can still live on today and push you towards actions that are not true to yourself and are hurtful to your spirit. If we are unaware of how our past is keeping us stuck, then we cannot move beyond it onto our path of self-progression. We will remain bound by the same destructive patterns that bring us here today.

Despite that other people impose some of the forces impacting on our lives, many are burdens we have created for ourselves—but only because we have not brought them into conscious awareness. In fact, without consciousness, we spend our days reacting to the whims of others and our passing ideas, as well as the images and messages we encounter in the media.

The first step then is to become aware of what you are buying into—what pressures are driving your actions and beliefs. Then, most importantly, tuning into the incredible power and wisdom within you that exists free from all the noise of reactive thoughts and actions.

'Awareness is the greatest agent of change.'
~ Eckhart Tolle

The first step then is to see beyond the haze and to get clarity about who you are and what drives you, and to understand the beauty that you hold within. That is why the first part of this book you're holding is called The Retreat. It invites you to a place of reflection and understanding. It helps you see all of the pollution that sits around notions of physical beauty and shows you the pure place of your potential. It provides the space and time to understand your beliefs about beauty, how much they influence you and what you truly believe about yourself in this moment. This is a process of retreat, moving inwards to a place of sanctuary where we can take the knowledge gained from the outside world and use it to understand what you truly value. It is a journey inwards to get to know the perfect seed within that exists no matter what is going on outside.

The Journey of Retreat

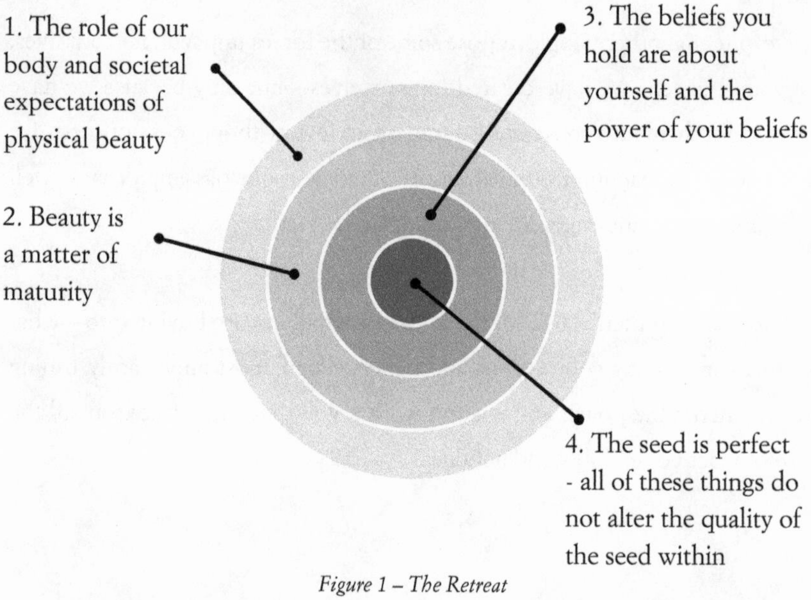

1. The role of our body and societal expectations of physical beauty

3. The beliefs you hold are about yourself and the power of your beliefs

2. Beauty is a matter of maturity

4. The seed is perfect - all of these things do not alter the quality of the seed within

Figure 1 – The Retreat

In this section, The Retreat, we will be discovering:

- The two fundamental roles our bodies play: as a home for our spirit and as the way we interact with others;

- Societal standards of physical beauty, where they come from and their potential to subdue our mind, body and spirit;

- How much the standards of others drive our thoughts, feelings and actions;

- Understandings of internal beauty—what it means when you hear that beauty comes from within;

- How beauty is a matter of maturity—becoming aware that there is no right or wrong view of beauty, but that it is a perception informed from a person's level of consciousness;

- What you believe about yourself and how these beliefs have shaped your life; and

- The fact that the past does not tarnish the seed within—the perfect beauty that you hold inside.

Courage

Secondly, with awareness comes great responsibility. Taking on the personal responsibility to be the best that we can be requires courage. Heading off on an adventure where there are considerable risks and so many unknowns takes great bravery, and also faith in oneself. Every great expedition needs to be founded on a solid base of self-awareness and skill. That is why the second part of this book, The Expedition, comes after The Retreat. Because only when you are aware of the forces operating around and within you, do you have the ability to deal with the clouds and stormy weather. Then you are ready to head forth on the adventure that is the blooming of your full potential.

Once we understand the seed inside, and how precious we are, then we are ready to bloom. This is a process of courage and constant dedication to practising self-compassion. It is a journey of care for our body and our mind, making sure our environments and actions help us bloom into our full beauty from the inside out. It is a conscious process where we decide what influences to subscribe to and which ones not to attune to. The Expedition is the process of living consciously, compassionately and confidently.

The Expedition

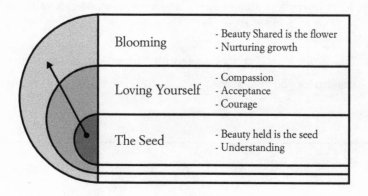

Figure 2 – The Expedition

We will move towards this place by discovering:

- What is self-acceptance and how it differs from self-esteem;

- What is confidence and how you get it;

- How you move from self-acceptance to self-compassion;

- Your physical environment and how it may be helping or hindering you;

- Your relationships and how they may be supporting or limiting your growth;

- The difference between caring for your body and caring about your body;

- How to care for your thoughts and feelings; and

- The care you provide that goes beyond your physical attributes (i.e., your spiritual health connects to your sense of purpose).

Moving Forward – Your Call

Here is the heart-filled love note kicker: While it is just so easy to talk about all of these wonderful things, the reality is that moving forward, creating change is not always easy. Looking inwards and confronting our self-limiting beliefs, past hurts and harmful habits is tough. Planting your seed in the right place and embarking on the process of letting your beauty bloom takes a tremendous amount of courage. There will be days where you feel incredibly powerful throughout this journey and other days where you will feel ready to pack up and head back to your little house with 'stuck' written above the door. Sometimes being stuck feels easier. Sometimes old habits, no matter how destructive they may be, make you feel safe. As the adage goes, it is better to be safe than sorry!

Only you can decide how important your freedom, your growth and your blooming are to you, and what you are willing to do to stay on this path. Only you can decide how important it is for you to live your best life and to finally love being you.

Moving Forward – My Story

I do understand that moving onto a new path is fraught with unknown feelings. It is the uncertainty of the new adventure that causes the most angst and is likely to be the most significant cause of inertia. So, perhaps my story might provide a little bit of insight into what is possible. I know all too well the suffering that you might be experiencing right now. I was always overwhelmed by unconscious habits that were holding me back in places of shame and unworthiness. Throughout my developing years, one particular boy excessively bullied me, and his taunts stung. At that time of my life, I was vulnerable and dependent upon the acceptance of others.

With the benefit of hindsight, I can now reflect and think, 'How dare he bring toxicity into my days by telling me I was a fat and an ugly whale?' 'How dare he make me feel unsafe and undesirable when what I needed the most at that time was love and support?' What made this worse was that the things I needed—acceptance, compassion and care—were also void in my home life. My upbringing in those years was not filled with love, joy, support, laughter or happiness. Instead, it was a massive current of fear.

Now I see that the lessons bestowed on me in my developing years had a profound and lasting impact on the way I saw myself. This, in turn, resulted in the lack of care I gave myself. I now understand how the torment of those daily words shaped my beliefs around who I felt I was and was not, and what I thought I deserved and did not deserve. But it was only through the process of awareness that I was able to start the healing process and reprogram myself with supportive beliefs.

I began to see the pollution around me, created by the churning and machinations of so many unhelpful beliefs and habits. Once I saw this toxicity from a bright space, I was able to begin asking fundamental questions in order to process change. Questions like: Was the beauty standard I saw on social media really what I wanted to achieve? Why do stretch marks have to be ugly or unfavourable? What was the cellulite on my body trying to tell me? Does it even matter if I have it? Is it really that bad? What kind of person am I really, beyond all the physical stuff? What is my purpose in this lifetime? What is my true calling? How can I make a real difference in this world?

As I began to question things, I started to be able to shift years of deep-rooted beliefs. I began to feel lighter in my body. I began to feel good from within. I was coming back home to myself. I had found that place of love, sanctuary and retreat and encountered the whole seed within— my true self. Knowing it is there and feeling its true nature, one can then be filled with the courage to share its beauty with the world. I genuinely believe in the beauty of that perfect seed that lies within you, untouched by the actions of others, unharmed by what may be many years of self-neglect. My hope is that this book will not only help you come home to your true beauty but that it will also help you find the courage to let it shine too.

Start a Ripple

This book is all about you and your blooming. There is no doubt about this at all. But I want to highlight that if you dare to move forward—if you have the bravery to understand and to shift unhelpful thoughts and behaviours—then you also begin a ripple. Every little action you take to be the best person you can, positively influences others. It flows out into the world and touches the lives of many. Some people, as we will see later in the book, will not like it at all. They may be threatened by your growth and push back against your ripple. But for every one of these people, there are many more that will be inspired by your actions.

You see, the fact that you are here—seeking a way to be at peace with your body and spirit—means that there are others out there doing the same. Many women you know are stuck, even if they may not show it. There are also girls out there looking for role models to show them how to live courageous and happy lives. If you choose to take the challenge to bloom yourself, then you are also shining a light on the possibility, and the process, for others. I know the thing is, you can talk to girls all you like about the importance of self-love and living to their full potential, but your actions speak much louder than your words. This is your chance to show them how. Your courage can be an inspiration and make a massive positive difference to the lives of many.

But it all begins with you.

AN IMPORTANT NOTE

Throughout this book, there are references to different concepts of physical beauty and body image. I know for some that this is an area of sensitivity and vulnerability. I know this because I have been there. I know that sometimes these discussions may trigger distressing thoughts or feelings.

If anything in this book brings difficulty for you, please reach out to one of the organisations in Helpful Resources listed in the back of this book. You have been so brave to begin this journey, so please be courageous and ask for help if you need it. You do not have to do this alone. These resources are there to help you work through any challenges you are experiencing and help you be the best you can be.

'Asking for help is not a sign of weakness;
it is an act of great strength.'
~ Suzzi Hartery

COMMITMENT STATEMENT

I commit to enter this journey with care
and compassion for myself and others.
I commit to taking responsibility for my health
and wellbeing and seeking any help I need
along the way.

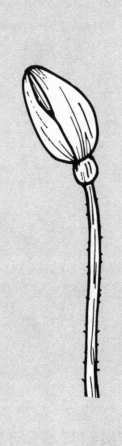

PART A

The Retreat –
Discovering Beauty
from the Outside

CHAPTER ONE
The Role of Our Body

Let's start things off with an important question: How often do you think about your body? I think it would be interesting to keep a tally of how many times throughout the day you think about your body. Perhaps it is the very first thing you think about as you get out of bed, noticing a sense of energy and excitement or heaviness and fatigue. Is it when you look in a mirror after your morning shower or are you thinking about your body when you decide not to look in the mirror that day? Maybe it is when you are dressing and noticing if your clothes feel looser or tighter. It could be when you pass a newsstand and see the latest fashion magazine, instantly noticing elements of the model's form or features you wish you had.

Do you think about your body when you exercise, and your body feels powerful or puffed or somewhere between? You may think about your body after a meal and notice the sensations of feeling comfortably full, uncomfortably full or still extremely hungry. Perhaps you also notice your body at night when you lay to sleep, feeling weary and tired or restless and agitated.

I suspect that either consciously or unconsciously, you think about your body a lot each day. Some thoughts may be positive and helpful, whereas others might be critical and hurtful. But how often do we stop and think about the role our body actually plays in our life? What is the purpose of our body? Of course, the most prominent function of our body is to keep us alive, but more profound than that it serves two equally important purposes:

1. It provides a home for our spirit; and
2. It is the way we interact with others.

A Home for Our Spirit

'The body is your temple.
Keep it pure and clean for the soul to reside in.'
~ B.K.S Iyengar

Much has been written about the mind-body connection. As we will see in upcoming chapters, there is a direct relationship between the state of our mind and our body, and vice versa. But the influence with the body goes deeper than just the mind. The body has a connection with our true essence, which is what you may call your soul, your spirit, your heart, your psyche, or what we will refer to as the perfect seed.

Your body is there to nurture the seed within, and to give it a safe home where it can develop, grow and bloom into its full potential. How we treat our body can work to support and energise this growth, or dull and suppress its existence. The reality of being human is that our bodies decline and decay year by year. It does not matter how much we may try to delay or mask the demise of our bodies, they come with a use-by date. The finality of this cannot be changed.

So the body is not an end in itself. It is a vehicle that we can use to help us reach our full potential in this life and make our unique difference in this world. It is a temple, holding the sacred relic of our soul. However, sometimes in our drive for praise or acceptance, we forget this vital role and treat it as if it is a slave to our will and not an enabler of our power. Jennifer Love Hewitt says it perfectly when she states: 'Remember, your body is a temple, not a 7-Eleven.'

In return, the state of our mind and our spirit directly affects the health of our body. Stress and anxiety have significant and detrimental health impacts, both internal and external. Beliefs of unworthiness can lead to a whole range of behaviours that seek to harm and punish our body, rather than support its vital and life-giving function. The struggles you are having right now with your body may be in part driven by the battles you are having with your mind and your unique spirit. Denying the needs of our body, shunning its role as a home for our soul, is also to disregard its power and potential.

How We Interact with Others

Often this first function of our body is overshadowed by a preoccupation on how we appear to others. There is no doubt that the body plays an essential role in how we interact with and are perceived by others, which we will deal with the opinions of others a little later. Here we concentrate on how our body can enable or damage our ability to form strong and positive relationships with others. Let me give you an example. Think about a person you know who is in touch with their true spirit. They are clear and confident in their life direction. You admire them for taking real care of themselves. How do they stand? How do they move? How do they sit? What body language is evident, and what does this tell you about them? How does being around them make you feel? How free do you feel to be yourself with them? How comfortable does it feel to be with them?

On the opposite end of the spectrum, think about someone you would classify as insecure, a 'follower' or someone who is wrestling with finding their place in this world. Someone who is getting battered around by the changing winds of other people's opinions and expectations. How do they stand? How do they move? How do they sit? What body language do you see them using? What does this tell you about them? How does being around them make you feel? Do you feel the ability to be your true self around them? Do you feel free to express your treasured beliefs and values? How comfortable does it feel to be around this person?

When the person you are with is being authentic, true to themselves and open with their challenges, then this calls you to be the same. Their sense of self gives you a place of safety where you can express your innermost desires and challenges. Their courage gives you the strength to ask for the help you need to move forward. This person creates a safe and nurturing home for others because they prioritise making their body a safe and nurturing home for their spirit. They have used their body to create a home in which their spirit can live freely and express itself in all of its bold beauty. Is this the role that you would like to play for others too?

No matter who we are, our bodies do the same thing. They thrive off nourishing food and feel good when we do things we enjoy. They have mechanisms like a beating heart to pump blood, lungs to help us breathe and a liver to filter toxins (plus so much more). Our body also has a beautiful mechanism called homeostasis that keeps your body in perfect balance. Where we differ is where our personality gets to shine. This is where we get to bring those unique traits and the things that help us express who we are to fruition— we do not have to see it as a way of standing out or feeling like we would not be accepted. We get to see it as a way of expressing our true self and permitting others to do the same.

The Relationship Between Roles

So, as you can see, the two roles of our body are not independent. They work together—first to create a safe and supportive home for our true essence, and then as the way we can step forth on our adventures. Your body provides the home for your retreat and then becomes a tool you can use to explore the world and live your full expression within it. In this way, the role of being a temple for your spirit is the foundational role of your body. When we work on this and create a strong foundation for yourself to shine, then you open the doors to an honest and positive relationship with others and yourself. Our ability to interact and to bloom into our full beauty requires this strong foundation.

The danger begins when we place a focus on the external-facing role of our body, without the base of understanding, self-acceptance and love. It is like building a house on sand. The house may look incredible, but it is vulnerable to the weather around it. Strong winds of other people's opinions or adverse events can make it break and even fall. A seed needs protection from the elements to be able to sprout confidently and grow into its full potential. A flower needs the support of strong and healthy roots to thrive. The same is true for the fantastic and beautiful seed that lies within you.

Let me share with you about a client I worked with and how we came to discover how her appearance represented the exact explanation above. She was self-conscious about her height, being on the shorter end of the scale. She is in a position of authority at work though and has to manage a huge team. Each day she goes to work wearing stilettos. She is known for her array of incredibly high shoes and is never seen without them. I know shoes are 'her thing', and I get that. I love shoes! But as our sessions uncovered, she could be seen wobbling around in the shoes. When she walked, it was with caution.

As we were talking, the image of this woman wobbly in high heels made me think of the situation we are in when we do not respect the role our body plays as the home for our soul. We may look the part, act the part and be seen to have all the confidence in the world. But in reality, every step we take is shaky and cautious. We have set ourselves up to be knocked over. So, how can you build a temple that is worthy of your unique and beautiful spirit if you do not start with a strong foundation? How can you move into this world if you spend your days worried about falling over? How can you express your authentic and unique beauty confidently if you do not have a safe place you know you can return to at any time for peace and strength? This is what I helped her uncover and I will for you too.

That is why the role of being at home for our authentic essence is the foundation. As such, if it has been disregarded in the past, it now needs to be given the utmost priority.

What Has Been Your Priority?

As we will see throughout this book, there is never any right or wrong. The only thing that matters is understanding where you are at right now, and making conscious decisions about where you want to be. So here is a critical question for you. Over the past few days, what proportion of your time has been spent...

1. Caring for and nurturing your body as a home for your unique and beautiful potential?
2. Concentrating on the way your body looks and moves in this world?

Perhaps you have been in an intensive retreat and have spent 100 per cent of your time on the first. Maybe you have been repeating or stuck, and so your focus has been on the second. Again, there is no right or wrong; just take a rough estimate of where your time has been spent lately.

Question: What proportion of your time has been spent...

Caring for my body as a home for my soul %	How my body looks and moves %	Total
		100%

Great work! Knowing it does not matter at all what the answer to the above question is. The fact is that you have stopped to think about it. You have shone a light on what you are currently doing, and begun to question whether this feels right to you. You have started to see the potential for other ways of being, and taken the first step towards making choices that are both conscious and that sit well with your body and spirit.

The inevitable next questions are:

- What do you think and feel about where your efforts have been invested in the past?

- Do you have a sense of what the key drivers have been for splitting your time this way?

- How has this split of priorities been working for you? What have been the pros and cons of this approach?

- Is there a difference you would like to make in your priorities in the future? Why or why not?

Important: Your Body is Not Your Only Tool

Of course, the purpose of this book is to help you make peace with your body and to bloom and shine. We will deal with many body related issues we can have throughout this book. Though, it is essential to remember that your body is not the only tool you have to express and make your difference in this world. There are three other essential tools that you have control over that are there to help you achieve your dreams and allow yourself to express your true self. These are:

- Your voice. Thanks to the world of the internet, we do not even have to be seen to make an impact. Through podcasts, blogs and social media, we have a voice. Our words can inspire others, and these channels can be used to bring your beauty, in the form of your thoughts and opinions, to the world.

- Your relationships. It is said that anything we can do ourselves is never big enough. People are also a valuable tool to help you be the best you can be. In no way am I advocating that people should be used as a means to get what you want. It is not like that at all. Relationships exist as a two-way street to help each other shine and to help each other achieve our unique potential. We will learn more about the importance of supportive relationships in Chapter 14.

- Your actions. Even more important than the words you use are the actions you take. Yes, your body enables your efforts, but you choose the actions you take. You may have built grand plans for your bright future, but if you take no action, then they are just wasted time. Likewise, the contemplation and understanding you will gain through reading this book is essential. Still, it is what you do with this understanding hat counts.

WHAT NEXT?

You have begun an incredible journey of understanding yourself and living consciously. This chapter introduced two critical functions of your body—being a home for your spirit and a way to interact with the world. We have seen how these roles are interdependent, and our ability to live freely is founded on the solid base of a loving home. If you have worked through the questions, you would have a sense of the role you have prioritised to date, and where you have invested your precious time and energy. You will have also had the opportunity to consider how well this current pattern is working for you, and whether you would like to make any changes in this area. Remember, there are no right or wrong answers here—only understanding and moving towards what is unique, beautiful and right for you.

With this understanding, it is time to dive into the role that is given so much attention in society. That is, the body as a tool to interact with the world, or, put more simply, on our physical appearance. Let us start with the façade of the house—the way we look to others—and check in on the plethora of expectations that others put on our bodies.

'The journey of a thousand miles begins with one step.'

~ Lao Tzu

COMMITMENT STATEMENT

I commit to becoming mindful about the role
that my body plays in my life.

I commit to being aware of how I care for
my body—a home for my unique and
beautiful spirit.

CHAPTER TWO

Beauty Standards and Where They Come From

Who Decides What is Beautiful?

Across the ages, there have been archetypes of what is deemed beautiful by society. But who decided what images were shown? Well before the rise of the media, these standards were a celebration of the natural female form. With the rise of a patriarchal society and the growing influence of the media, the tables were turned. We were shown every day what beauty is for their society and in their time.

In the ages before print or electronic media, the artists decided what was beautiful by their choice of subject. It was the sculptors and painters who captured the female physical form that was looked upon and admired by others. I cannot profess to know what was in the minds of ancient Greek sculptors or renaissance painters. However, art historians tell us they were recording and honouring what they saw as 'the divine'. They were capturing nature in all of its true splendour.

With the creation of autocratic societies, those in power decided what was deemed as beautiful. One only has to look to one Emperor's declaration that lotus feet were beautiful to see a trail of torture that was imposed for centuries. One decision about what constituted beauty led to the subjugation and impairment of generations of women.

When photographs and print media became available, society then became exposed to all of the images that the media bosses decided to print. Of course, these images have always been of royalty. As we will see, the pictures of Queen Victoria and her maternal figure became the standard to which so many women aspired. Corsets and wireframes became the method by which women could emulate the most powerful woman at the time. Some things have not changed here, with magazine covers flooded with images of, 'Look at how much weight she has lost,' to, 'Look how much weight she has put on.' It's an endless battle of playing with your confidence and, for many like us, a topic that's taboo to talk about. Playing on the thoughts of, 'I do not like my body.' So, let us change and pick it apart.

Paparazzi and media bosses will tell us that they continually publish these images because it is what their readers want to see. But the counter-argument is that readers are groomed to want these pictures by the hype that the media puts around them. Research was conducted in Fiji that clearly showed the introduction of television had a significant and negative impact on the body image of the women and girls that were exposed to it[1].

The Effect of Mass Media

We all probably understand in theory that mass media, especially television, movies and social media, play a massive role in creating and encouraging standards of beauty. The study that was conducted in Fiji shows the real impact. Researchers visited one region of Fiji in 1995. At this time television was not available in the area, and there were no reports of dieting to lose weight. The researchers returned to the area three years after television was introduced and again surveyed the female population. After the advent of television, almost 70 per cent of girls reported they were dieting to lose weight. Also, girls coming from families with a television were three times more likely to have harmful attitudes towards eating. Similar results have been found right across the world in different cultures such as Singapore, Japan and Ghana.

This behaviour change in such a short time is alarming. However, remember that this increased preoccupation with body image eventuated just because of television. Surveys of American schoolgirls showed that magazines also create a concerning response. Almost 70 per cent of elementary schoolgirls surveyed reported that pictures in magazines influenced their view of an ideal body shape. Nearly half (47 per cent) disclosed that the pictures made them want to lose weight[2]. It is distressing to think of the pressure felt by women today thanks to social media, with idols and influencers in front of them constantly.

You could argue that with the advent of social media, the decisions about what is beautiful is very much delegated to every individual. Each of us can look at Instagram pictures, watch YouTube and TikTok videos and make our own decisions about who we resonate with and who we admire. We can believe that we have our own free will to follow who we want and celebrate what we genuinely believe is beautiful. To some extent this is true, but there are two critical things to remember when you see the subscriber/follow numbers:

Corporations are funding the most popular with their own agendas. There could be thousands of people doing the same thing on YouTube, but the ones that get sponsored—the ones that get paid to do it—are those who 'fit' the image that the sponsors want. So in reality, the most popular are not always those with the best message, but they are those that support a brand image.

There is the reality of groupthink. I watched a fascinating experiment where teenagers were asked to rate a singer's performance. Of course it was a set-up, and the performance was very amateur. All it took was one kid to voice critical feedback, and every other participant followed to mock not only the performance but the performer as well. If some of the people in the room wanted to give some support and encouragement, it never got to see the light of day. It was drowned by the loudest voice, and the need to fit into the group. So, the message is not to think that everyone buying into or outwardly supporting what is being advertised as beautiful really believes it. Perhaps they are just doing what is entirely reasonable for us humans—seeking the security of a tribe.

The Fickle Nature of Beauty Standards

To understand just how beauty standards work, and how fickle they can be, let us have a look at how they have varied across the ages. As you will see, the beliefs around what constitutes physical beauty have changed so much across time. They also differ greatly depending on your ethnic culture. There has never been one universal standard that defines beauty across the ages or the cultures. The definition of physical beauty has been shaped by the context of life, the wealth and food available and, more importantly, in our modern world, by the messages broadcast by mass media. Today, beauty standards have become far less defined by the environment in which we live, and more dictated by the commercialist motives of cosmetic, fashion and media companies. The beauty standards are far less driven by what is healthy for a woman, and more about what 'sells'. Let me show you how.

Through my research for this book, I had known that the standard for physical beauty has fluctuated throughout time. Still, I was even surprised when I mapped the estimated ideal weight for a woman over time.

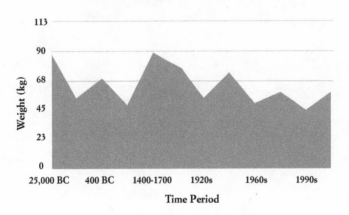

Figure 3 – The Average Ideal Weight Through The Ages

What alarms me the most is that looking at this graph, it mirrors my battle with weight fluctuations throughout my life so far. Yes, like many women, I have put my body through much stress riding the weight roller-coaster. But what this graph does show is just how variable the expectations of a woman's weight have been over time. To meet the standards of physical beauty across the ages, you would have to go from maternal in Victorian England to pencil-thin in the Roaring 1920s. Then back to full-figured and curvy for the Golden Age of Hollywood, and then to extreme thinness for the heroin-chic days of the 1990s. Just imagine how much of your life would be taken up with trying to meet the ideal body shape of the time. Let's dive in a little more and look at some examples of what was motivating each era.

Pre-History (25,000 BC)

One of the oldest known sculptures of a woman is called Venus of Willendorf, which was made around 25,000 BC. There is debate as to who made the icon and what it was used for. What we do know though is that this image comes from a time when people were battling for daily survival. The Earth was in the midst of the Ice Age, and all inhabitants were fighting with cataclysmic climate changes. Food was scarce, and each day would have been a struggle for survival.

For this reason, it is unlikely that this sculpture would have been a self-image. It is more likely that it would have been a representation of an 'ideal' physical state, representing abundance, fertility and the hope of a plentiful future. In this way, the image is opposite to the reality the sculptor may have been facing at the time. Interestingly, the Venus of Willendorf is also an image from societies that had not become patriarchal, which was estimated to have occurred around 10,000 BC.

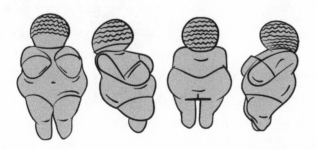

Ancient Egypt (1000 BC)

Figure 5 – Nefertiti 1345 BC

In Ancient Egypt, women enjoyed many freedoms, including land ownership and even being able to become Pharaohs—one of the most famous being Nefertiti. Her depictions show the beauty standard of the time being thin (but not excessively so), with a high waist and slim shoulders. Interestingly, this sculpture would have shown Nefertiti after going through one or more of her six childbirths. At this time, due to the proliferation of agriculture, food had become more bountiful. Yet, we see that the standard of beauty has become the opposite to the availability of food. While there was a wealth of food, the value of beauty was placed on being slim, as if it depicted the importance of the values of discipline and restraint.

Ancient Greece (400 BC)

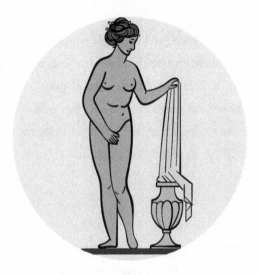

Figure 6 – Aphrodite of Knidos 400 BC

By 400 BC, civilisations had become well and truly patriarchal. Governments were formed and communities were built around producing and selling agricultural products. More importantly, exploration, expansion and wars were occurring, which shifted the power balance to men. At this time we have Aristotle recorded as calling the female form 'a deformed male'. So this is some indication of what women began battling with as the world became more male-dominated. Women were shamed for not looking like men. There were very few depictions of women early in Ancient Greece, as the preoccupation was with the perfection of the male form. The first one we see that gives a glimpse of the revered form of women was the Aphrodite of Knidos. The image shown of this goddess is one that is plump and full-figured, again depicting the female form as one offering abundance.

Han Dynasty (200 AD)

Chinese societies have been predominantly patriarchal since ancient times, which meant that they were very much subject to the dictates of men regarding standards of beauty. To be beautiful in the Han Dynasty meant you had to be delicate and slim, as well as have pale skin, long black hair, white teeth and tiny feet. What are known as 'lotus feet' were deemed to be the height of beauty in the 10th Century. These were feet shaped like moon crescents, and no larger than 11 centimetres.

This, of course, is entirely unnatural, and so to achieve this state of excellence, girls' feet began to be bound when they were toddlers. They continued to be bound so that their toes wrapped around and their feet were stunted. You would not believe it, but this practice began when the Emperor's favourite concubine bound her feet to dance on a lotus flower. He loved it, and so binding feet was seen as a way to ensure favour with the Emperor. There were grave physical effects of this practice. Women ended up with infections, broken bones and very much housebound, ensuring their chastity.

By the middle of the 17th Century, the only girls without bindings were from the poor rural tribes and women who worked in fishing because they needed healthy feet to balance on boats. However, the cruelty of this practice continued for more than a thousand years up until it was actively forbidden in 1949.

Figure 7 – Depictions of Beauty in the Han Dynasty

Figure 8 – The Practice of Foot Binding to Create Lotus Feet

Italian Renaissance (1400–1700)

Figure 9 – The Birth of Venus 1480 AD

Things were very different for the women in Renaissance Italy, and yet the standard of beauty imposed on them was also determined by wealth and men. Any value that women held was only concerning the men in their lives, either being God, their fathers or their husbands. So a woman's appearance was used to signal the status of her husband. A rounded body, full hips and large breasts indicated the abundance and wealth of the husband. Pale skin indicated that they spent their days sheltered rather than labouring in the sun, and high foreheads showed intellectual astuteness. This model is no better demonstrated than in the famous Botticelli painting from 1480 titled 'The Birth of Venus'.

Victorian England (1830–1900)

Figure 10 – Queen Victoria

Queen Victoria was the most famous figure of this era, and she prided herself on not only being the Queen but a wife and mother as well. She placed great importance on the family and motherhood, and so it is no surprise that the beauty standard was full-figured. However, to accentuate the female bust and hips, corsets were worn to pull in the waist. Cage crinolines were also worn, along with layers of petticoats to create the hourglass shape, which became the fashion of the era. Doctors counselled against tight-lacing the corsets, due to the restrictions placed on respiration and the possible damage to internal organs and fertility. Yet the erect, almost military-style posture the corsets created, was believed to reflect a moral and well-ordered society.

What's important to note here is that corset-wearers were having their ribs displaced and their lungs squashed, making it hard to breathe. Their hearts were being compressed and struggling to pump and their stomachs crushed, making eating a nutritious meal incredibly difficult. One Victorian lady was reported to have said: 'I had only eaten two bites of my biscuit [and] there was no room beneath my corset for a third.' It is not surprising that women of this era were known to faint regularly. Between malnutrition, low blood sugar and a lack of oxygen, staying standing would have been a challenge. This did not stop corsets being introduced at a very young age to help girls 'train' their waists to meet the desirable shape.

Figure 11 – Corsets Were Used for 'Waist' Training

Journalists mocked the frivolity of women who were willing to sacrifice their health to be bound into tight corsets. In the *Chicago Tribune* in 1891, it was stated that 'It is difficult to imagine a slavery more senseless' than the wearing of tight-laced corsets. But women themselves also battled against the trend. The Victorian Dress Reform Movement arose in the middle of the Victorian era. It advocated for a change to fashion, saying that it restricted women's ability to participate in society. Namely, corsets, crinolines and petticoats made it difficult for women to move freely and impeded their ability to work for wages. Corsets made them physically dependent and subservient to men. This, then, was the beginning of the women's emancipation movement.

Roaring Twenties (1920s)

Figure 12 – Women Were Engaged in the War Effort

What a difference a world war can make! Between 1914 and 1918, the world was in the grip of the First World War. So, what did they need lots of to make their weapons? Steel. What were women's corsets made from? Steel. So, amazingly in 1917, the War Industries Board asked women to stop buying corsets so that the steel could be used in the war effort. It is phenomenal to think that in this one step, 28,000 tonnes of steel was saved, which would have been enough to build two battleships!

Also, with the men away in the war, women were needed to build the battleships. Long hair was impractical, and short hair became a symbol of freedom. Hard work and a lack of food took its toll on women's bodies, and so gone were the expectations of full figures. The standard of beauty in the 1920s was a combination of practicality and the ravages of war. It was symbolised by short hair, a flat chest and a thin boyish figure. This was also the time that Lucky Strike cigarettes began marketing to women, using cigarettes as a symbol of freedom and a slimming aid.

Figure 13 – Actress Claudette Colbert, 1920

The Golden Age of Hollywood (1930–1950s)

Figure 14 – Marilyn Monroe, Elizabeth Taylor and Bette Davis.

After World War I, came a time of plenty, and there was a boom in the filmmaking industry. Of course the filmmakers were men, and so they determined the look of women that would make it as 'stars' and as the standards of beauty for this age. Curvy bodies and thin waists were back in as the screens and magazines were graced with pictures of Marilyn Monroe, Elizabeth Taylor and Bette Davis.

The Swinging Sixties (1960s)

Figure 15 – Twiggy Depicted the Beauty Standard of the Swinging Sixties

After World War II, women's place in the workforce had become enforced, and they were able to make choices for their lives other than being a mother and housewife. There was a push towards peace, freedom and youth. Twiggy was the most famous model at the time and came to depict the age of the Swinging Sixties—tall and thin again (like the 1920s). Corsetry had become a thing of the past, and in fact, freedom meant not having to wear bras at all. However, there was one significant beauty trend that became more pronounced during this time, and that was the preoccupation with youth. Fashion designers had been for years driving trends to more youthful designs, and now, with Twiggy, the look was complete. The standard of beauty was now a child-woman and pixie-like.

The Excessive Eighties (1980s)

Figure 16 – Cindy Crawford, Christie Brinkley and Jane Fonda

The 1980s are known predominantly for one thing: excess. So many opportunities had opened up in business, and people were making a lot of money. Women were going into business too and had their own money to spend on designer clothes. The age of the supermodel had begun, and so had the age of aerobics. While the beauty standard of the eighties was still tall and thin, it shifted to become more muscular, tanned and buxom.

At this time, television was becoming a regular part of households, and more and more women and girls were being exposed to the supermodel images on television and in magazines. Cindy Crawford, Christie Brinkley and Jane Fonda were the stars of the moment, and the dieting and exercise industries encouraged other women to be just like them. It is no surprise that the 1980s saw a significant increase in the eating disorder anorexia nervosa. Women had the beauty standards in front of them every day and were being actively marketed the means to achieve them.

Heroin-Chic Nineties (1990s)

Figure 17 – Kate Moss Became the Face of the Nineties

After the greed, waste, hedonism and materialism of the 1980s, there were many disillusioned youths. All of these excesses had not brought the happiness they had promised. By the time the nineties rolled around, this disillusionment was manifesting in music and addictions. In the 1990s the fashion trend became 'heroin-chic', which was personified by emancipated, withdrawn and pale women. Kate Moss was the model of this age. In 1997, thirteen designers went public to denounce the use of the heroin-chic image and declare their concern with the effects of its glamorisation[3]. They recognised the influence that the images portrayed in the media and fashion industry and went public to call for a more responsible influence. This bold move sparked considerable criticism and debate within the fashion industry about the role it plays in the health and wellbeing of women.

Fast-Change 2000s

Four things characterise our current time. These are:

1. Rapid change—technology and trends can change overnight.

2. Social media—these trends are broadcast through and fuelled by the instantaneous nature of social media.

3. Consumerism—we are taught that if you do not like what you have or if something does not work, just throw it away and get another one.

4. Perfection—no longer do we have to be satisfied with either a full figure and an ample bosom, or a flat stomach and a small bottom. We now have the means to have it all. Body-sculpting exercises, body-shaping clothing and plastic surgery make any combination of physical appearance possible.

It is challenging to keep up with all of the latest trends in physique and fashion, and that is just the way that the beauty companies like it. In the industrial era, the main problem businesses faced was how they could produce enough cars, fridges, televisions and kettles to meet demand. Now, with our advanced manufacturing technologies, the problem instead is how do they sell all that they can make. The solution? Rapidly changing trends that encourage a throwaway mentality and pushing perfection.

Kim Kardashian is an idol of the current time. She epitomises the standard now of being skinny but healthy, having large breasts and bottom, but also a flat stomach. For the vast majority of women, if they choose to buy into this ideal, much time, energy and money are required to transform their natural shape to meet this ideal.

Figure 18 – Kim Kardashian Represents the Beauty Standard in 2020

For example, when a plastic surgeon was asked, based on photos, what work Kim Kardashian has had done, he suggested a long list, including:

- Chin, cheek, jawline and lip fillers;

- Anti-wrinkle injections;

- Multiple Brazilian butt lifts;

- Liposuction;

- Breast implants and;

- Rhinoplasty.

It appears that Kim may agree with the sentiment, having been reported saying: 'My body is a temple, and my temple needs redecorating.'

Tell me, were you shocked with the thought of the torture women went through in China to get lotus feet? How is the surgery done to transform a woman's body shape these days any different? Could I suggest that the only difference now is that we have an anaesthetic to knock us out during the surgery, and painkillers to help us through the discomfort of recovery? I wonder if plastic surgery would be so popular if we had to live with the hurt of the moment and the pain in the process?

Beauty Across Cultures

Just as the concept of physical beauty varies across time, it also differs across cultures. In the previous section, we have seen what the ideal of beauty is in the western world. However, if you were to head into Asia or the Middle East, there are very different standards. For example, in western cultures tanned skin is the preference, indicating a life of wealth and leisure. However, in Asia and the Middle East women seek to lighten their skin, as paler skin is a sign of aristocracy and not having to work out in the sun. In these countries, women are preferred to be delicate and demure rather than the fit and toned physiques valued mainly in western countries.

The ideal of beauty, though, is very different in African and Polynesian cultures where curvy or 'big' is beautiful. In these countries, food can be very scarce. So as we saw with the very first female idols, larger women are associated with fertility, abundance and wealth.

This norm seems unbelievable in the western world, where eating disorders are continually rising. The rate of eating disorders has doubled since the 1960s and is becoming more prevalent in younger age groups. The National Eating Disorders Association of America (NEDA)[4] reports that 40 per cent of nine-year-old girls have admitted to dieting already. Some five-year-olds have also expressed concern about their body image and the need to diet to stay thin. Also, 40-60 per cent of elementary schoolgirls (ages six to twelve) are concerned about their weight or about becoming overweight. Our western world is driving our girls to hurt themselves, and to deny their pure spirits in the pursuit of a beauty standard that is not realistic. These standards are created only for the self-serving ends of the advertisers and sponsors that pay for the images we see. And it will be noted that those mentioned are simply the main representation of the time and not a posing judgement more to help you understand and visualise the key beauty standards of that time.

Conclusions on Beauty Standards

So as you can see, the ideals and standards of beauty change throughout time and across cultures. While globalisation and the internet are harmonising tastes and ideals, there is still not one set standard. If anyone asks you who is the most beautiful woman in the world, the answer would be 'it depends'. The judgement of physical beauty depends on what part of the world you are from.

Hopefully, what this chapter has also shown you is that standards of beauty are manufactured. They are determined mainly by the ruling class—the wealthy—those who have time and choose to spend their money chasing ideals. These may be people in the ruling class such as the emperor in the Han Dynasty, the casting agents and producers responsible for choosing the stars of the stage and screen, or those choosing the fashion models of the time.

I cannot profess to know the motivations and intentions behind the beauty standards each one has promoted. All I know is that there's an increase in physical manipulation, emotional distress and psychological illness from the marketing of unnatural or extreme beauty images. The standards that have been set appear to have very little to do with a woman's health and wellbeing, and more to do with the achievement of commercial success. It is for these reasons, and to give you every chance to grow and bloom into your unique beauty, that you need to understand your beliefs.

Because your beliefs of beauty are the only ones that truly matter!

What is Your Reaction?

Now it is time to take a step back. Look back on all of those standards of beauty and how much they have changed over time. Review the results of the research, which clearly show the impact that the media has on our beliefs, thoughts and behaviours. Also scroll through any Instagram, YouTube and TikTok accounts you may have, and contemplate the following questions:

- How do you feel when you see each of the beauty standards across the ages?

- What is your reaction to these images? Do you feel drawn in by them, repulsed by them or somewhere in between?

- What are your thoughts around the study that was done in Fiji?

- How much do you think you might be influenced by the images and 'influencers' around you?

- Why do you follow the women you do on social media? What are the qualities or characteristics about them that you admire? Do you think that they influence your beliefs or behaviours in any way that is good or hurtful to you?

There is just one critical note for this exercise: You must not judge yourself for any thoughts you have. Just be aware of them. This is another bold step in becoming conscious of ideas that may be preventing you from feeling free in your own body. It is not an exercise in criticising yourself. It is an exercise in becoming more aware of how you think and act. It is only with this awareness that you have the power to change any beliefs and behaviours that are not serving you.

WHAT NEXT?

We have seen how standards of physical beauty have changed over time and differ across cultures. We have investigated how the media influences beauty standards and how we, in turn, are influenced by what we see. The result is that loving ourselves and our bodies is not as straightforward as it may sound. The displays and pressures of 'perfection' are everywhere. Advertising, our peers and sometimes our own family can push for us to meet standards that are just not natural, or healthy.

So, we can now recognise and understand the crazy world of physical beauty standards we see around us. It is entirely up to us, though, how much we subscribe and buy into these archetypes. Before we begin to define what beauty means for us, let us look at the one other contributor to our views of beauty—our level of maturity.

COMMITMENT STATEMENT

I commit to observing consciously the beauty standards advertised by others and how they influence the feelings I have about my own body and appearance.

CHAPTER THREE
Beauty is a Matter of Maturity

What is Beauty?

'The beauties of the body are as nothing to the beauties of the soul.'
~ Plato

For thousands of years, philosophers have contemplated the question, 'What is beauty?' They have pondered what it is and what it is not. They have reflected on where beauty comes from and how it changes over time. They have documented its blessings and its dangers. After all this dedication of mental effort, what is the result? What is the answer?

The answer is that there is no answer. All we are left with are many different opinions and perspectives, many of them conflicting. Here are just some of the diverging views about beauty developed over the ages:

Beauty is…

a physical characteristic	versus	an internal virtue
an objective quality	versus	a subjective judgement
a set of defined proportions	versus	an evolving attribute
the cause of desire in others	versus	the creator of confidence in the self
something you have	versus	something you experience
found alongside harmony	versus	something you experience

Interestingly, most of these notions of beauty were formed by yet again, men. However, one woman had a vision of how these disparate views fit together. Diotima was an ancient Greek prophetess and philosopher who greatly influenced the concepts of beauty and love espoused by Socrates and Plato. She saw that there is an evolution—a path of maturity along which people progress in their understanding of beauty. She called it the 'Ladder of Love'.

The Ladder of Love

Diotima's Ladder of Love explains that initially, people seek beauty in the physical form. In step one, there is an attraction to physical features, particularly of one person. As a person expands their knowledge and awareness, he or she progresses to step two and can begin to see the beauty in all bodies. They begin to appreciate physical features that are different from the original thoughts. As greater wisdom and maturity is gained, the understanding of beauty shifts from the external and physical realm to the moral and spiritual. Here, at step three, it is recognised that physical beauty is both meaningless and impermanent, unlike a person's spirit or soul or seed. At this stage, beauty is seen in the mind and heart of a person, not just in their physical appearance. This is the vision of beauty that Plato describes as the 'beauties of the soul' and believes that these well surpass any beauty held in the physical form.

'Beauty is not in the face; beauty is a light in the heart.'
~ Kahlil Gibran

Ultimately, at the highest point of this ladder (step six), people understand the beauty that is beyond words. They can see and feel the beauty in all things. In this final level of maturity, beauty is appreciated to be both immortal and divine. It is unchanging and eternal. Both Plato and Plotinus supported this view, believing that as a person experiences more of life, the multiplicities of views on beauty fall away. The person understands that beauty is not confined by the boundaries of our conception or our language.

Diotima's Ladder of Love

We focus on the physical beauty of one person.

We appreciate the physical form more generally.

The beauty of the soul outweighs the beauty of the body.

We appreciate the practices and customs built by the people with beautiful souls.

The thirst for knowledge - not only about the world and others but, most importantly, about ourselves.

We understand the beauty that is beyond words. We see and feel the beauty in all things.

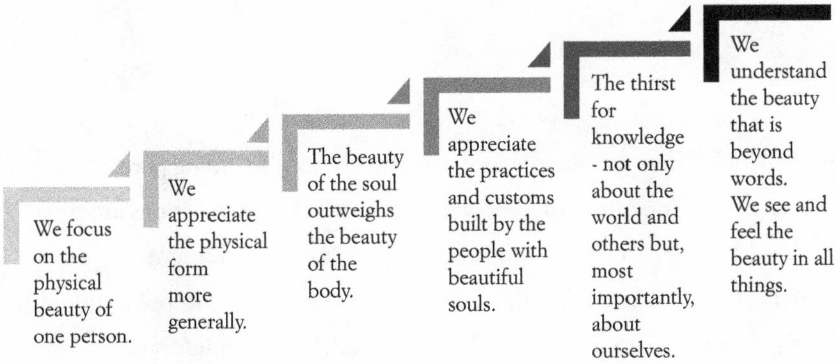

Figure 19 – Diotima's Ladder of Love

Arriving at this point, however, is not just a matter of time and age. There are two essential steps along the way, being:

- The appreciation of the practices and customs built by the people with beautiful souls (step four); and

- The thirst for knowledge—not only about the world and others but, most importantly, about ourselves (step five).

The key message here is that there is no right or wrong when it comes to understanding what beauty is. The real answer to the question, 'What is beauty?' is 'it depends'. It depends on where you are at in your life journey. It depends on how you have been shaped by the masses of life experiences you have had to date. It depends on the places you have lived, as well as the people you have grown up and spent time with. It depends on how much you have embedded yourself into the world of modern media, and how much you have pursued the path of self-knowledge.

Levels of Consciousness

Dr David Hawkins developed the same notions of maturity much more recently. While not specifically targeted towards understanding perceptions of beauty, he developed a model showing how our beliefs and actions are driven by how developed our consciousness is. His 'map' of the levels of human consciousness is also called the Scale of Consciousness. He used extensive testing of patients using Applied Kinesiology (AK) to determine how a person's level of consciousness coincides with their perceptions about themselves and their lives. Below you will see the Levels of Consciousness, as defined by Dr Hawkins[5].

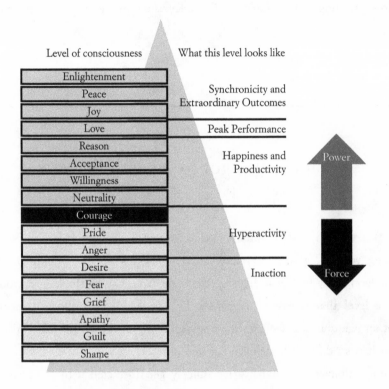

Figure 20 – The Levels of Consciousness by Dr David Hawkins

Noting the importance in being aware that the lower levels of consciousness are not lesser or worse than those at the top. The lower levels are fundamental to learning and growth. They are essential to experience in order to be able to progress to the heights of the human experience. They are part of what we must work through to become our best selves. It is the pain of these lower levels that provides the desire and drive to move forward.

Dr Hawkins' model shows the separate steps to enlightenment and that they have one great divide: between force and power sits courage. Everything below represents destructive and harmful behaviour that uses force on others to achieve its aims. Every level above courage is life-promoting, encouraging and supporting a life of integrity. These levels tap into a person's own power to thrive.

What has this got to do with Beauty?

Believing in and blooming into your unique beauty is a process of loving yourself. But if you look at Dr Hawkins' model, you might be wondering why love is so high up the scale. You may be thinking it would be a level that is easier to achieve. Dr Hawkins' description of love is not an emotion or a feeling, but a way of being in this world. He explains that it is so difficult to achieve because our society is so obsessed with the physical domain. As humans, we quickly get distracted with the physical domain and the realm of reason, which concentrates on form, not substance.

According to Dr Hawkins, most people aspire to the level of pride. Pride is undoubtedly the level we see enacted by most of the celebrities and influencers around us. Pride feels so much better than shame or guilt. However, it is a false feeling of strength, as it still relies on external factors such as wealth, position or power, and holds it by exerting force onto others. Courage begins the levels of empowerment because this is the first stage in which people are not taking energy from others and begin to take responsibility for their own growth and success. It is at this point that a choice can be made about how to respond to our situations. It is at this point that we can decide and act on our values and beliefs around beauty.

The move to neutrality is characterised by becoming flexible, relaxed and unattached. You feel safe in your skin and no longer have anything to prove to other people. However, while this may be a nice place to be, especially compared to where you currently are, it can result in complacency. The move to willingness then is one of acknowledging your abilities and becoming determined to put them to good use. Acceptance then is the recognition of your role in the world, the ability to see the big picture of your life and the start of setting and achieving goals and living consciously and proactively to deliver on your potential.

It may be easier to understand the difference in these levels of consciousness by working through an example. Let us utilise one most you would be familiar with: starting a new diet. Many different levels of consciousness can drive the motivation and intention behind this act. For example, if you are teased regularly about your weight or figure (this was absolutely me), then you may be prompted to start a diet from a place of shame. The motivation is felt as a force upon you to fit in and to adopt other standards of physical beauty. But what if this same action came from a place of reason? What if, instead, it was driven by the recognition that your diet of food and exercise was essential for your physical and mental wellbeing? What if it was motivated by the desire to become the best you can be? In this latter scenario, dieting is a means of living up to your real power. So while two people may take the same action, it is the intention and energy behind it that determines whether it gives life or destroys your energy.

Stages of Adult Development

There is one more maturity model that is directly related to our ability to appreciate and bloom into our beauty. That is the Theory of Adult Development by Dr Robert Kegan. This model presents maturity as a shift away from reliance on others' opinions, and towards an independent sense of self. There are five stages of the Theory of Adult Development, which are:

- Stage 1—Impulsive Mind (early childhood)

- Stage 2—Imperial Mind (adolescence, 6 per cent of the adult population)

- Stage 3—Socialised Mind (58 per cent of the adult population)

- Stage 4—Self-Authoring Mind (35 per cent of the adult population)

- Stage 5—Self-Transforming Mind (1 per cent of the adult population).

The stages most relevant to us are two to five. While most relevant in childhood, Stage 2, the Imperial Mind, is essential to understand as it provides a view of what lower levels of maturity look and behave like. Even if it is not directly relevant to you, it is helpful to be able to detect in others around you. In Stage 2, the prime concern is the person's own needs and interests. Any relationships are only formed to get what the person wants, and so are very much transactional in nature. People at Stage 2 will follow along with societal standards, rules and trends not because they believe in them, but because they fear external punishment, or desire external rewards.

In Stage 3, the Socialised Mind, our concerns move away from our own needs to how others experience us. In fact, in this stage, we tend to take on too much responsibility for how others see us. Stage 3 is where we transfer the views of others onto ourselves. The ideas of those around us become most important, and we take on external thoughts and beliefs as our own. Ultimately, in this stage, a person does not have a strong sense of an independent self and spends much time living up to the expectations of others or society. Because of this, they are continually seeking out external validation for a sense of self and worth. In Stage 3, we allow ourselves to be defined by our family, society, ideology or culture.

It is a big leap from the Socialised Mind to the next stage, Stage 4, being the Self-Authoring Mind. In this stage, we are no longer defined by our environments, but take on the responsibility to define ourselves independently from the expectations of others. We no longer take on others' opinions as our own. We develop our view of the world and create our counsel, authority and voice. Rather than seeing others as the 'cause' of our emotions, we take responsibility for our feelings and actions. Most importantly, at this stage, we recognise ourselves as an ever-changing being. We appreciate that we are not fixed in body or mind and that we have the power to create the life we want to live.

Stage 5, the Self-Transforming Mind, builds upon this understanding of empowerment, going further to release us of all expectations around our identities. We see the complexity and continual changes in our lives. We can reinvent our identity to expand ourselves and take on new challenges. While in the previous stage, we were willing to question authority, in Stage 5, we are also ready to question ourselves and see ourselves from different perspectives.

Dr Kegan's theory focuses on how to grow up and become an adult. However, reading through the descriptions of the stages, many higher-level characteristics reflect a goal of becoming free of the opinions of others. Moving up the stages of adulthood means becoming more self-aware, having a greater independent sense of self and being able to manage the social influences upon us.

We cannot appreciate our unique beauty if we are stuck in Stage 3 and care most for acceptance and fitting in. We need to have a strong sense of our power, our values and our beliefs to be able to enact them and to let our genuine and unique self shine. We cannot bloom if we are going to let others dictate what is beautiful for us. Defining ourselves and breaking free of the expectations of our environments is essential to making peace with our bodies, and is a crucial trait of Stage 4 adult behaviour.

So how do you progress to the higher stages of adulthood? The answer is the two things we covered in the introduction: consciousness and courage. We need to be aware of what we believe, think and feel, because for so long we have taken on the opinions of others and our voices may have been lost. Achieving consciousness is a process of asking yourself questions. Questions are a great way to stimulate interest and curiosity in who you are and what is important for you. That is why each chapter of this book ends with a set of questions—to help you foster your individuality and nurture your internal voice.

Questions will help you become more aware of what you are thinking and feeling. However, it takes courage to reflect critically on how well your current behaviours and thought patterns are serving you. Courage is required to answer the questions honestly and to be open to the fact that you may not like some of the answers. It also takes courage to identify areas of growth and even more to take action to make this growth a reality.

What These Models Mean for You

Here is a visual summary of how the two models, the Levels of Consciousness and Stages of Adult Development, relate to each other.

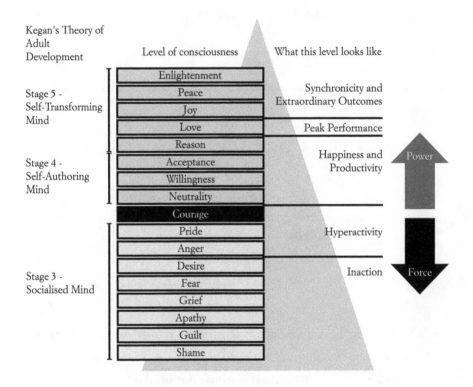

Figure 21 – The Levels of Consciousness and Stages of Adult Development Models

All these maturity models show that accepting yourself, loving yourself and feeling joy in your skin requires moving away from shame, guilt and fear. Blooming into your unique beauty takes great courage and effort, a shift away from the preoccupation with the physical form and a focus on your own opinions and internal sense of direction.

Moving forward requires a great deal of energy. It takes effort, assistance and a willingness to be open and honest with yourself. The human brain is very good at preserving energy. So, it is understandable that people get to the point that works for them, and then the force of inertia gets them stuck there. While the model may show you where you may be stuck now, it also shows clearly what your potential is. It is in you to move from inaction to happiness—to move from impulsive and socialised to self-authoring and self-transforming. It is my aim that this book and the work you will put in along the way will be your guide to help you live from your incredible spirit and use this to bloom in this world.

What These Models Say About Others

'Everything has beauty, but not everyone sees it.'
~ Confucius

While thousands of years of thought have explored the intricacies of differing opinions of beauty, it has not resulted in one definitive answer. It is important to remember that there is no single dogma, directive or regulation dictating what beauty is. You are entirely free to decide what beauty means for you. Additionally, everyone else has the same freedom. You have seen how many different perspectives on beauty there are. Therefore, it is inevitable that along the course of your life journey, you will meet people whose notions of beauty differ from yours.

There are so many examples of this from my life. Being excluded from school groups and teams because I was not 'pretty', being teased and mocked for being ugly or too loud and having boys refuse to kiss me in a game of spin-the-bottle. I remember once a then close friend wrote a two-page letter to a boy I had a crush on about why I was not worthy of him. Crushing and heartbreaking I know! I had not yet even puckered up the courage to talk to this boy, so he probably didn't even know who she was talking about. But thanks to the knowledge I have now, I understand this behaviour was not about me, but a function of her understanding of beauty. You see, when people present judgements about your physical beauty, they are sending loud and clear messages that:

- Their minds are placed at an immature understanding of beauty. There is nothing wrong with this—it is just an indication of where they are at in life; and

- They are uncomfortable with being outside the 'norm'. They are more concerned with fitting in and being part of a 'tribe' than they are with exploring the unique gifts of each person.

It must be said that if you are the one making critical judgements about your physical beauty, then this also holds true for you. Again, there is no right or wrong here, just an understanding of where you are at in your journey.

It may be argued that visual media such as television and film have concentrated the view of beauty to its most basic form—the preoccupation with physical beauty. That it has played a significant role in standardising our opinions of what physical beauty looks like. I find it interesting that the Disney princesses we grew up with are lauded for their beautiful hearts. Yet, each one still has been given perfect proportions, long flowing hair, flawless skin and a remarkable singing voice. Social media only proliferates these views. Again,

I'll restate here, how we are exposed endlessly to people who have achieved fame and fortune because they fit the mould of what 'society' deems as beauty.

Remembering, this merely represents someone else's opinion of beauty. And they are entitled to have it, just the same as you are entitled to define what beauty means for you. At the end of the day, it is your opinion that matters, as you have to live with yourself every day and rest with your consciousness every night. Here is the kicker—the big-hearted realisation—you ready? When you are home alone in your comfy clothes and you are drifting off to sleep each night, external physical beauty holds no relevance whatsoever. There is no-one else to view and judge your body or your facial features, so for all practical purposes, they cease to exist. There is just you, left with what truly matters and what endures well past any physical state.

Where Are You Now?

So, just as Dr Kegan suggested, let us get curious about ourselves and dive into some questions and critical reflection.

Firstly, think about three scenarios or events from the past few days or years that often go in merry-go-round thoughts in your mind. They may be because they were pleasant and happy times, or because they provided some difficult challenges for you. Try to find scenarios that involve different groups of people. For each situation, ask yourself:

- What level(s) of consciousness was I acting from during this event?

- What stage of adult development did my behaviour look most like?

Secondly, do you find yourself behaving at different levels of consciousness or adult development with different people? For example, do you act with a Socialised Mind and out of fear or pride with one friend? However, with another friend, do you find yourself more empowered and motivated to operate with a Self-Authoring Mind? This difference is significant to note now and will be explored further when we investigate relationships that can help or hinder our growth.

Lastly, identify what level of consciousness and stage of adult development you would like to be operating from. Why? What are your motivators for wanting to be at this level?

WHAT NEXT?

Throughout this chapter, we have begun to understand the reasons behind different perceptions of beauty. There is no right or wrong when it comes to perceptions of beauty, just a matter of maturity. There is no judgement about where anyone, including yourself, is with regards to the level of consciousness and stage of adult development. As individuals, we are shaped by many influences, and each of us has a unique past that has created the place where we find ourselves today.

We have learned that the movement between maturity levels could exacerbate struggles you may be having with your body. Movement between levels is tricky and takes a conscious process of analysis and reflection. Moving forward with care and attention will allow these transitions to be times of peace and strength.

But before we think of moving forward, we need to go a little bit deeper into the process of retreat. We need to delve into and understand the beliefs and opinions we have about ourselves right now. We need to get intimate with what we believe, think and feel about ourselves. It is time to strip away what others are telling you about yourself and listen to your own heart. I am giving you permission to ignore the voice of others for a little while, and listen to your voice. Let us find out what it is telling you.

COMMITMENT STATEMENT

I commit to bringing awareness to my current
level of consciousness and maturity, and how it
may be helping or hindering my relationship
with my body.

CHAPTER FOUR

How Do You See Yourself Now?

Start Where You Are
– The Gift of Self-Awareness

'When you know yourself, you are empowered.
When you accept yourself, you are invincible.'
~ Tina Lifford

We have spoken already about the perceptions of others, but how it is only your opinion of yourself that truly matters. Before you can move forward, you need to understand where you are right now. I can tell you over and over again that you are perfect, but until you experience it—until you feel it inside—they are only words. You need to understand what the voices in your head are telling you that may be helping or hindering this complete view of yourself. You need to understand the stories that are shaping your days.

This, dear friend, is where this journey moves from being theoretical to being real. It moves from thoughts to feelings and ideas to experiences. In this chapter, you call on your courage to open your heart and become aware of how you see yourself right now. So let's start really diving into these two very important questions:

- What do you think of yourself?

- How do you feel about yourself?

Self-awareness is the ability not only to see yourself clearly, but to have a full and frank insight into how you think about yourself. Most importantly, though, the process of self-awareness and the self-knowledge that results needs to be free of judgment. Your thoughts and feelings about yourself are not right or wrong; they are just an indicator of where you are at right now. They are your starting point on this incredible and exciting journey home to your true and full beauty.

Let us take an example. Say through this process of self-awareness, you identify that you see yourself as 'broken'. That you do not have what it takes to form a meaningful relationship. Okay, so this is pretty stinky thinking. It certainly is a self-limiting belief. But what if you start piling self-criticism on top of this? What if you start telling yourself that you are pathetic for thinking this way and that you should be stronger than this? Well, now you are just heaping toxic self-criticism on top of thoughts and feelings that in themselves would already be creating so much self-harm. We will talk about the role that your judgements play in Chapter 16. But for now, just remember that when you identify your current thoughts and feelings, they need to be devoid of judgement and attachment. They are not good or bad. They just are, and they certainly are not you. They are just thoughts and feelings—that is it.

Enter this process as a curious scientist, seeking great insights into yourself. Come into the search for self-knowledge with as much objectivity as you can muster. Judgements only cloud the clarity we can gain about our current situation. Research has shown that when we see ourselves clearly (without the clouds of judgement), we can be more confident and creative. We can make better decisions, communicate more effectively and form closer relationships.

The Two Types of Self-Awareness

So, let's investigate two types of self-awareness here. These are:

1. Internal self-awareness. This is an understanding of our inner landscapes. How we feel, what drives and motivates us, how we feel in our environments and the view we have of our impact on others. Internal self-awareness is also how well we understand our strengths and weaknesses. This type of self-awareness is linked to greater relationship satisfaction, personal and social control, as well as happiness. It is negatively related to anxiety, stress and depression.

2. External self-awareness. This is how well we understand how others perceive us. When you know how others see us, it is possible to be more empathetic towards them and more accommodating of their perspectives and opinions. When you understand how others see you, it opens the doors to more honest communication in all your relationships, which is further empowering your true self.

Dr Tasha Eurich has created a set of four archetypes that describe the characteristics evident, depending on the level of proficiency at both internal and external self-awareness[6]. Take a look below and ask yourself "Where do I see myself on this grid at the moment?"

External Self-Awareness	Internal Self-Awareness
Low	High
High	High
Low	Low
High	Low

Introspectors
- Clear on who they are
- Don't identify blind spots by getting feedback from others

Aware
- Clear on who they are and what they want to achieve
- Seek out and value opinions of others

Seekers
- Don't yet know who they are or what they stand for
- Don't know how others see them either

Pleasers
- Focus on how they appear to others
- Overlook their own needs and fulfilment

Figure 22 – The Four Self-Awareness Archetypes by Dr Tasha Eurich

Upon reflection, I discovered I had always been a pleaser. I was so attuned and sensitive to the needs and expectations of others that I lost connection with what I needed and what was important to me. From this position, I realised that if I genuinely wanted to be open and free, then I must invest in reconnecting with who I am and what I care about. Given there have been decades spent pleasing others, this journey to becoming fully aware has been a process of experimentation, reflection and learning. It is achieved through listening to our internal dialogue and our deepest feelings and also seeking feedback from people we can trust.

Self-Awareness Versus Self-Consciousness

While self-awareness is essential to your ability to bloom, there is a caveat: Beware of crossing the boundary between self-awareness and self-consciousness.

Self-consciousness is when self-awareness becomes an obsession, and when you become preoccupied with yourself and how others see you. This can create concern over the gaps you see between where you are and where you want to be. Self-consciousness can result in shyness and acute social anxiety, and inhibits your ability to reach your full and beautiful potential.

This tendency to notice and focus on ourselves and our failings is completely normal. It is due to what is known as the Spotlight Effect. Very simply, the Spotlight Effect is the way our brain works to make us think that everyone is looking at us and that we are the centre of attention. The Spotlight Effect begins to play a crucial role in our lives in the pre-teen years, when our social awareness expands. We become more concerned with what our peers think of us and about fitting in. It originates from our days living in tribes, when to be ostracised would have meant being outcast. Living in a tribe, we had to worry about our image in the minds of a few key people in the tribe—those that decided who could stay and who would receive food and shelter. However, these days, with social media, we have to worry about being embarrassed in front of the whole world. This has made the Spotlight Effect even more influential.

Well, here is a pin to burst your bubble of inflated self-concern: The fact is that no-one cares what you do now or the humiliating things you have done in the past. Phew! What a relief right? This is because they are living within their own spotlights—viewing themselves as most important—with their thoughts mostly centred on themselves. Do you not believe me? Two excellent studies have proved it. In the first, a student was sent into his college lesson wearing a Barry Manilow t-shirt. Surely he would be laughed out of the classroom? Less than half of the students even noticed he was wearing it[7].

In the second study, called the 'Bad Hair Day Study',[8] students chose either to pay more or less attention to their hair. When other people were asked about their hair, there was minimal perception variation from day to day. The study showed that people do not notice when we are looking our best or when we are looking our worst. Most are far too occupied with their own problems and concerns about how others see them. You may be worried about how your hair looks, but others are more worried about their own hair! Most of the time.

So, now that you are aware of the Spotlight Effect, I hope it will be easier to avoid slipping into the realm of self-consciousness. Self-awareness can liberate and lift you to where you need to be. Self-consciousness only brings you down and can make your current challenges feel even more challenging.

Describe Yourself

So, let us begin. Let us plant your seed and make growth with the beginning of your great journey. Let's weed through and tackle the first question together 'How do you see yourself now?' To help, in Appendix 1, you will find a list of words that you can use to describe yourself. Some have been classed as helpful as they empower and enable. These are called strengths. The other descriptions are categorised as problematic because they can be used to judge and limit your self-belief, confidence and potential. These can be called weaknesses.

Work through the list of descriptors in Appendix 2 and circle those that you would use to describe yourself. Circle those that you believe apply from both the helpful and problematic sections. Just remember, this activity is all about how you see yourself. Be sincere and honest. This is the starting point to letting your true beauty bloom, so please treat it with the respect, kindness and honesty you deserve.

Now, take a step back and look at your list and ask yourself the following questions:

- What is the balance between helpful and problematic descriptors you have chosen for yourself?

- Is your view of yourself weighted on either side?

- Are you surprised by some of the things that you admitted you believe are your strengths or your weaknesses?

At this point, you might want to walk away for a moment to create some space for reflection. Take a breath, smile, touch your heart or give yourself a great big internal hug. You have begun to reveal your truth. This takes courage. So, just in case you have not already, you better go back and circle courageous!

'Owning our story and loving ourselves through that process is the bravest thing we will ever do.'
~ Brené Brown

Feelings About Yourself

The words you have chosen to describe yourself are the 'what' of how you see yourself now. But there is another crucially important step in the quest to self-awareness, and that is having an understanding of the 'so what'. Each one of these thoughts you have about yourself has implications for how you feel about yourself. When you think that you are any of these things, feelings arise. These feelings have driven your actions to this point. They have created a myriad of experiences throughout your life, from the joyous to distressing, and everywhere in between. Self-awareness is the process of connecting what you think about yourself to how this makes you feel. So, let us take this next step and bring your self-awareness from words into sensations.

Go through the list of descriptions you have chosen and for each one, complete the sentence: 'When I think I am [insert descriptor], I feel [insert sensation, feeling or emotion].' To help out, Appendix 2 contains a set of emotions that may help you identify what is going on in your mind and body. Knowing, your thoughts and feelings work together to make you who you are. This exercise is so powerful at showing you how they are serving or not serving you right now.

Have a look over the feelings and sensations that resulted from the way you described yourself. Generally, do they fall into the category of 'force' from the Levels of Consciousness? For example, fear, grief, anger or shame? Or are the feelings more of love and peace? There will be a mix of both every day but see at this time if there is one place you tend to be the most in the levels of consciousness described in Chapter 3.

Feeling Discomfort

It is inevitable that through this process of becoming aware, you will stumble across thoughts and feelings that range from uncomfortable to deeply painful or sad. Unfortunately, the existence of hardship and difficulty is a reality of life that we must learn to deal with. It is never the existence of discomfort that is the problem. It is how we choose to deal with it when it arises that defines us. Living through and learning through these feelings only brings you closer to your authentic expressive self.

'A seed neither fears light nor darkness, but uses both to grow.'
~ Matshona Dhliwayo

In saying this, though, many of us are not taught how to do this. We are not instructed on how to deal with uncomfortable or painful feelings as they arise. We will delve deeper into feelings in Chapter 17 but until then, if this exercise does bring up emotions that are distressing for you, it is vital to get support. A list of people you can contact can be found in the helpful resources section of this book if you need to talk to someone about what you are experiencing. Do not go through this alone—there are so many people out there who want to help—including me.

How Others Behave

This chapter has concentrated on gaining an understanding of how you see yourself now. It has helped you gain some sense of your starting point on this journey. However, it must be stated that the models you have used to increase your self-awareness apply to everyone else around you too. When you encounter difficult people or destructive behaviour, know it is a function of their current level of self-awareness and consciousness. Just as your current situation must be treated with care, respect and understanding, so does theirs.

Please do not use this information to pigeonhole or judge others. Please use it to improve your acceptance, tolerance and compassion for others, just as you are doing for yourself. We are all at different levels of consciousness and are functioning at the level of knowledge that we have obtained. Judgement or criticism of others who are operating at lower levels will certainly not help them. It will only bring negativity into your life. A much better use of your precious time and energy would be to seek out people at higher levels of consciousness than you so that you can learn, grow and bloom! Claire Nuer, a Holocaust survivor, says it best when she states: 'The only way to create love, safety and acceptance is by giving them.'

WHAT NEXT?

Going through this exercise, you have now come to a place of great intimacy with your true beliefs and feelings about yourself. Some of these feelings will have created much hope and enthusiasm, while others may have created a sense of despair. It is futile to shy away from those areas that create discomfort, as ignoring them or suppressing them only fuels their power. If you want to move forward and bloom, then the only way through is by acknowledging, understanding and neutralising those beliefs that are there to serve you.

You have come such an incredible way in acknowledging the helpful and not-so helpful beliefs you have about yourself. Now, let us understand where these beliefs have come from so that we can begin to challenge those that haunt us and heal the wounds that they have caused.

COMMITMENT STATEMENT

I commit to being honest with myself about my
self-image, and to understand that this is just my
beginning point and does not need to be my future.
I commit to treating myself with kindness,
acceptance and love.

CHAPTER FIVE
You Are Planted in Your Beliefs

'It's what you choose to believe that makes you the person you are.'
~ Karen Marie Moning

There is no doubt in my mind that the seed within you is perfect. I hope that the past few chapters have shown you that the point at which you find yourself now is just that—a point in time. So much energy has been invested in getting you here in whatever form the 'here' takes for you, and it comes with so many opportunities. Now, if you want to move forward, to grow and bloom into your beauty, then it is a matter of focusing your energy to surround yourself with the things that will help you bloom.

For a plant, the soil is vital. It creates the warmth, chemicals and nutrients to start the germination process. If the acidity of the earth does not suit the type of seed, then the seed will not germinate and will stay dormant until it is planted in the right soil. It is the same for the seed held within you. Instead of soil, though, your seed is planted in beliefs. The nature of the beliefs you hold will either support your seed to sprout or keep it trapped. Beliefs can hold the seed tightly and strangle it or create a warm and nourishing home from which it feels confident to move forward from and spring to life.

Beliefs go by many different names, including principles, theories, views, dogmas, opinions, codes, standards or tenets. Whatever name they go by, beliefs are incredibly influential. They determine not only your thoughts and emotions but also actions. By understanding your beliefs, you can see how they may be helping or hindering your progress to being the person you truly want to be. As we have seen in the first section of this book, working with your beliefs is a process of awareness, understanding and compassion. Only by having the courage to look deeply at your beliefs are you able to see those that are helping you live up to your full potential and those that are stopping your growth.

What Are Beliefs?

Beliefs have driven every single thought and feeling you have had and every single action you have taken to this point in your life. The way that you view yourself, your life and those around you has also been shaped by your beliefs. As you will see in the next chapter, your beliefs are incredibly powerful. First, though, it is essential to understand what influences your life now and your future.

Beliefs Can Be Encoded

While beliefs are held in our minds, they can be encoded into laws, rules, stories and practices and passed down through generations. Many of the fables we were told as children encapsulate beliefs. The old story of the hare and the tortoise presents the moral that 'slow and steady wins the race'. It teaches the belief that quality and care is more important than speed. Even the clothes you find in shops have so many ingrained beliefs. Have you noticed that there are only dresses sold for women? Why? Well, it is based on the belief that men do not wear dresses. Have you ever stopped to wonder where this belief came from? Yet, there it is, ruling our choice of clothes every day.

Beliefs, if left unchecked, can also have detrimental impacts on our body and our overall health. Let me give you an example of family mealtimes. My grandparents lived through some incredibly difficult years. They grew up in the country during World War I, and the Great Depression and jobs were scarce. This meant that so was food, and things like butter and sugar were a luxury. When World War II came around, they were raising children and their prime focus was on making sure they had enough food to feed their children— my parents. School uniforms and books came second place to bread and meat. When a meal was placed on the table, you ate it all because you never quite knew where your next one would be.

My grandparents and parents grew up being told to eat everything on their plate. You weren't allowed to leave the table until you had. This belief that you must eat everything you were served remained even when food became plentiful. I remember seeing my father at the Sunday roast lunch ending up so uncomfortable—overfull from a huge meal. The belt would be loosened, followed by a nap to sleep off the excess. I grew up doing the same thing— finishing everything on my plate—even if I was full.

The consequence of this was that the natural signals of hunger and fullness were constantly being overridden. You ate when dinner was served, hungry or not, and you ate everything you were given, plus dessert, even if you were full. This belief and this behaviour meant I lost touch with my body and no longer heard the messages I was being sent about what it needed. I understand how food beliefs began for my family. But continuing them unconsciously in a time and place where they are no longer relevant can be unhelpful.

I know first hand that it can be difficult to change embedded beliefs, but with attention, care and a true respect for your body and your spirit, it is possible. Now, in my home, instead of demands made at the table such as, 'Finish your dinner,' there are questions like, 'Are you full?' My father still stuffs himself far too full at each meal, but that is his journey. I have chosen something different for my family and me. While I've chosen to see and do the work, I'm also very thankful for those who have gone before me.

Beliefs May Not Be True

While beliefs act as our truth, they are not necessarily based on reality. In fact, a person can hold a belief firmly, despite there being evidence to the contrary. For example, the idea that you are not beautiful can be firmly stuck in your mind, and for you, it has become a fact. However, it is contrary to the science of neuroplasticity, which provides evidence that you can change your beliefs with the right instruction, practise and reflection. With commitment and action, you can find and express your unique beauty.

Just look at the beauty standards that we saw in Chapter 2. The beliefs that people held around beauty were not based on any 'fact' but only personal opinion and whim. They shifted and changed throughout time with no concern for how they were harming our health and wellbeing. The medical advice was that women were being injured and malnourished from corsets, and yet they continued to be worn. Women underwent tremendous pain and suffering from lotus feet, and yet the binding continued. Women suffered through anorexia nervosa and other eating disorders to match the unrealistic body standards of the eighties and nineties, and yet they continued. It is only with the truth, and your willingness to confront it, that you can challenge unhelpful beliefs.

Beliefs Come in All Sizes

There is no limit as to how big or small beliefs can be. They may be as all encompassing and existential as whether you believe in a higher power or God, or as 'trivial' as whether you think red underpants give you more energy. Beliefs can be incredibly specific—for example, that you should not cook with olive oil. Or they can be as broad sweeping as suggesting that only women should wear makeup. Beliefs can also be directed at yourself, such as the belief that you are a great singer. But other people can also be the subject of your beliefs—for example, that your colleague secretly got a breast enhancement. Large or small, existential or mundane, specifically targeted or directed at the whole world, we are surrounded by beliefs of all shapes and sizes.

Beliefs Can Be Embedded

Some beliefs that you might have could be merely superficial thoughts that are readily changed. Trying on a new dress, you may at first believe that it does not suit you. But moving over to a mirror, with a change in perspective, you see that it really does complement your figure and your skin tone. The nature of these beliefs is transient and mostly harmless. However, other beliefs held are so deeply rooted that they have become part of our identity. They become embedded and non-negotiable. Take, for example, a vegan friend who believes whole-heartedly that humans should not be eating animals. No amount of discussion, science or marketing will ever change this person's mind as this belief has become interwoven with their personal identity and a representation of who they are.

These more deeply held beliefs have both pros and cons. They add value to our lives by helping us shape our values and find our place in this world. They define who we are, what we stand for and who is in (and out of) our 'tribe'. They help us make everyday decisions about where we go, who we spend time with and what we do. On the flip side, such rigid beliefs create a potential for conflict with those holding embedded but opposite beliefs. While one person may have the set belief that diet and exercise are all that is needed to lose weight, another may hold the belief of the importance of hormonal, mindset, stress and biochemical insights. It is not the existence of these beliefs that causes problems. It is the rigidity to which they are held and defended as 'right' or the only way. Inflexible beliefs that have no understanding or compassion for other viewpoints can be harmful.

Where Do Beliefs Come From?

Even though you are all grown up and making your own life decisions, you may be surprised to learn that most actions you make are based on beliefs you learned when you were a child. The thing is, as a child, you were incredibly open and vulnerable. You relied on the adults around you for survival. So this meant that you looked at what they did and said, learned what was acceptable and not, and absorbed all of these experiences into your own set of core beliefs. It was not only the beliefs of our parents that we adopted but also those of our teachers, childhood heroes, authority figures and governments. As a child, it was clear that these adults had it all figured out. We were under the assumption that they had all the answers and so what they believed must be right.

But where did the people who shaped our childhood get their beliefs from? Well, they would have been operating from a mix of:

- Universal beliefs—founded on knowledge gained over time. For example, excess sugar consumption contributes to developing diabetes. Likewise, your parents and grandparents were not privy to the level of knowledge we have now about many things. So the universal beliefs in their time would have been different. For instance, only now are we seeing fashion models with disabilities, Down Syndrome and embracing all body types. Decades ago, this would have been shunned and shamed. It does appear that general beliefs around beauty are changing, and there is a greater universal acceptance and appreciation for individuals of all shapes and sizes.

- Cultural beliefs—specific to a culture, background or faith. For example, some tribes in Africa and South East Asia use stacks of metal rings to stretch a girl's neck due to the belief that elongated necks are beautiful. In the coastal regions of Papua New Guinea, girls' faces were tattooed to signify their transition from childhood to a marriageable age. It is also clear that there are very different standards of beauty between Polynesian nations and Asian cultures, such as Japan and China. Where you grew up definitely has a significant impact on what you view as beautiful.

- Individual beliefs—held by one person. The people who raised you had their own unique set of beliefs formed from their family history, life experiences, education and personal values. Likewise, your own adventures in this life so far would have created a set of beliefs that are meaningful for you and influence the way you see and interact in this world. For example, when I was younger, I believed that all fats and oils were 'bad' because they would make me put on weight. Now, after understanding the nutritional needs of our bodies, I understand their important role and believe that certain fat types play a vital role in the health of our body.

So here we are, as adults, with our own existing set of beliefs created from the complex interplay of early authorities and our own experiences. Thanks to the internet, we have all the information we could ever need at our fingertips. We have also had the benefit of personal experience for many years and learned the approaches that seem to help our lives and those that seem to bring greater difficulty. We no longer rely on any other adult for our survival. So now is the perfect time to reflect on the core beliefs you hold, how they have shaped your life so far and if they may need to transform to support you in sharing your unique beauty with the world.

Beliefs Can Be Manufactured

There is one incredibly important point that must be made about beliefs: they can be created or changed through marketing. We have seen that what we believe is beautiful has been manufactured by marketing companies for their own gain. Marketing is an incredibly powerful tool. It can shift opinions and influence action to things that benefit companies, but can harm the individual at which they are targeted.

There is no better example than the way that processed foods, especially those high in sugar, have been marketed. In the book *Salt Sugar Fat: How the Food Giants Hooked Us*[9], we learn how Frosted Mini-Wheats were advertised as 'brain-food'. This distracted people from the fact that just one serving was providing one-quarter of an adult's sugar needs for the day. We also see the extraordinary lengths Coke went to in order to get kids 'hooked' on the high-sugar soda as young as possible. Coke was priced low to be affordable for children going to the corner store with their pocket money. The drink shifted from being sold in cans with 9 teaspoons of sugar to half-litre bottles with around 15 teaspoons of sugar. It was put in dispensing machines offering cheap supersize drinks with the single aim of getting people to drink more Coke. These 'double gulp' cups held almost 2 litres of Coke and about 44 teaspoons of sugar.

Coke was also ruthless with its advertising, having a huge presence at major sporting events. This was to ensure that people began associating Coke with memorable moments. What is most disturbing was that all of these activities were not done to build loyal fans; they were actually intended to build a tribe of 'heavy users'. These processed food giants use every trick in the book to get you addicted to their products. The results are alarming. In 1958 less than 1 per cent of the population in the United States had diabetes. By 2019 it was 10.9 per cent[10]. This is an increase of more than 1000 per cent in the space of only sixty years.

This example is indicative of the influence that marketing has over so many aspects of your life, including your beliefs around beauty. Knowing now that beliefs can be manufactured by others for their own gain, with no care or concern for your wellbeing or the welfare of the other people they are targeting. You need to be aware of how others may be trying to shape your beliefs and make you part of their crowd.

When Beliefs Create Conflict

It's likely that you have only considered your beliefs when conflict has arisen with friends or family. It is generally only these times that differences in core beliefs become apparent. This is clearly seen in the fights between parents and children in adolescent years. The child believes they should be able to make their own decisions and take the risks that will help them learn. The parents believe the child is not yet old enough to make wise decisions and, as such, may restrict their activity.

Even when there are different beliefs about the role of women? Some traditional parents push for a female child to limit career aspirations and concentrate on family duties. This can cause conflict with the daughter, who believes women can do anything and has no desire to become either a wife or a mother. Here a person has a choice: abide by the beliefs of those around them or choose a different path.

Any decision to give in to the beliefs of others and follow paths that do not feel right to us creates a massive conflict in our own hearts and minds. We will see this in Chapter 7 in the regrets of those who are dying when they express remorse that they did not follow their own dreams. Living with the conflict between your own dreams and the beliefs of others is draining. Now is the starting seed sprouting, with your opportunity to investigate your own heart, your own mind and your own convictions and let them shine through so you can live a life without regrets.

When Beliefs Unite

While embedded, extreme and inflexible beliefs can create conflict, there is an exciting opportunity that beliefs create for your journey. You see, beliefs also bring people together—into friendships, social groups, networks and organisations of all types. When you are clear about your beliefs and are dedicated to living them, then joining with others sharing these beliefs can be a vital source of energy and support. We can achieve amazing feats as individuals, but we can achieve even more with the hearts and minds of others who share our beliefs and vision for the world.

While the journey through this book is an individual one, you will be encouraged to seek out your kindred hearted community—the people and relationships that will help bring your beauty to life. Once you become aware and understand what is in your heart, and how you see the world, then there is great benefit in finding others to share your journey with. Your work throughout this book will change you, and with others, you can change the world for the benefit of girls, women and all of humanity now and in the future.

The Wisdom of No Blame

Throughout this chapter, thoughts may arise about beliefs that were imposed upon you that have impeded the way you have functioned in the world to date. You may be tempted to fall into the trap of looking back and blaming parents and peers for the difficult situation you may be in right now.

Let me give you an example from a friend. When she was in primary school, she always wanted to do ballet. But her parents, who were workaholics, saw dance as a frivolous exercise and a waste of money. Because she was termed 'pudgy' by them, they also believed she would look silly in a leotard and would be teased by the others in smaller bodies. Their beliefs meant that she did not get to pursue her dream of dancing. Sometimes she feels furious about this and would love to be able to blame them for her being classed as an overweight teenager. Maybe if they had let her dance, she would have lost weight and been healthier and happier at school.

Ultimately, though, looking back and judging someone else's beliefs and actions does not help at all. In fact, it is just wasting your precious energy. As we will discuss in Chapter 8, here is the opportunity to let go of the past and move towards your incredible future. But to do that, you need to use the 'wisdom of no blame'. In the past, you were reliant on the beliefs of others, but now you are not. You are a grown-up and responsible for your own future. Bring awareness of how your life has been shaped to this point, bring acceptance and understanding, and show compassion to others and yourself so that you can move forward. Use the wisdom of no blame and move towards the future you want. It is time for you to find the soil that will help you grow and bloom.

As an aside, my friend has been doing adult ballet lessons for a few years now and loves it! While in most lessons she feels quite out of place, she is learning and laughing along the way. Her bravery has shown me that it is never too late to pursue your dreams.

Let Us Analyse Your Beliefs

We only really see our beliefs in action when they are either uniting us with others or when there is conflict. Think about a time recently when you were getting along really well with someone—when you were 'on the same page' and the relationship felt comfortable and smooth. What beliefs did you have in common that enabled you to get along so well? Were these beliefs embedded or core values for you, or were they more superficial or temporal beliefs that brought you together?

Now think about a situation where you were in conflict with another person—when you disagreed with their views or perhaps felt misunderstood. What were the underlying beliefs that differed between you that may have been fuelling this conflict? Were these beliefs embedded or core values for you, or were they more superficial or temporal beliefs that drove you apart?

Now, take a look back at the beliefs about yourself that you identified in Chapter 4. Where do you think these beliefs have come from? Are they:

- Passed down through generations or a part of your culture? For example, you could have been taught that being slim is beautiful. This may have been explicitly stated, or you may have seen your grandmother or mother dieting or reacting to images in magazines or on television.

- Based on the opinions, judgements or standards of others? In the past, did someone always tell you that you were clumsy? Did a rumour go around a party that the boy you liked thought you were ugly? Or in reverse, did your teachers and peers tell you that you were kind, smart or beautiful?

- Founded on your deep-held values and life experience? For example, have you learned from your own experiences that you really enjoy helping others? Do you genuinely believe in the importance of being healthy or learning something new every day?

Take some time to determine if the beliefs you hold are driven from your own values, or are based on those told or taught to you by others.

WHAT NEXT?

We have seen that the beliefs you hold about yourself and your body come from complex interaction teachings from others, as well as your own deep values and meaningful experiences. Ultimately, though, they are the cause of where you are today. While their existence and their influence may have gone unnoticed until now, by understanding, questioning and shaping your beliefs, you can also create a new future. The beliefs you choose to keep and those you choose to discard will either enable or inhibit the thoughts and actions that can free you to make peace with your body and bloom.

Let us continue on and see how these beliefs exert such incredible power over your life to date and in the future.

COMMITMENT STATEMENT

I commit to entering my journey with the wisdom
of no blame. Instead of blame and criticism,
I will invest my energy into creating the soil that
will help me to grow and bloom.

CHAPTER SIX

The Power Beliefs Hold
Over You Now

'You are what you believe yourself to be.'
~ Paulo Coelho

The biggest single barrier preventing you from accepting and fully loving yourself right now are the beliefs that you hold. Your beliefs are creating your reality right now. If you look in the mirror each day with disappointment, then it is because you believe beauty is something other than what you are seeing. If you go to bed at night exhausted from trying to please others, then it is because you do not believe you are worthy just as you are. Beliefs hold an incredible amount of power over us and, more than likely, you may not even be aware of some that exist. But now it is time to bring them out of the shadows and see which ones are serving you, and which ones are preventing you from being the best you can be.

Beliefs hold incredible power not in themselves, but in the cascade of thoughts, feelings and actions that they create. The diagram below shows how beliefs have created the cycle of your life to date.

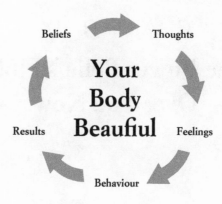

Figure 23 – The Self-Fulfilling Action Cycle

Beliefs Affect Your Thoughts and Feelings

The beliefs that you hold affect your thoughts and your point of view. The perspective you hold then becomes a means to judge yourself and others. For example, if you believe Barbie or a specific Instagram influencer is the expression of physical beauty, then you will use this standard to judge the women around you based on their physical appearance. The beliefs you hold also affect the choices you make. Two people could start a diet—that is, change their behaviour—but can be motivated by two very different beliefs. One person could start a new diet because they think they are not beautiful and need to meet the standards they see in the media. The other person could diet (or what I love to call nutritional intervention) because they believe they deserve to be fit and healthy and that their physical wellbeing is essential.

Beliefs Affect Action

Beliefs affect both the action you take and the results. Say you start a nutritional intervention, and so make a change in your behaviour. If you start getting results, such as your clothing fitting less snug, this can either:

- Begin to change the belief that, 'I am not beautiful,' because you are becoming closer to what you believe is beautiful; or

- Reinforce the belief that your health matters and that you deserve to be fit, strong and healthy.

But what if you do not get the results you are looking for? This can either:

- Foster the belief that it takes a lot of work to be beautiful, and this can drive more extreme behaviour;

- Reinforce the belief that, 'I will never be beautiful, so why both trying.' This continues a cycle of self-sabotage and self-destructive behaviour; or

- Reinforce the belief that you take action that supports your health. While there might be feelings of disappointment, the action continues because it is the right thing to do for your wellbeing.

Beliefs Affect Results

Beliefs can also directly affect results. Have you heard of the 'placebo effect'? It is known most widely in the medical field. Placebos are substances prescribed to patients for the psychological benefit rather than for any physiological effect. Still, they are told it is helpful in some way, and some patients actually achieve positive results. Their medicine may be a sugar pill, but the patient is not aware of it. In their mind, their 'medicine' is an effective treatment for their condition. So, while they are consuming an ineffective treatment, they believe that it has a supportive outcome and their body responds accordingly. Is that not incredible? That our beliefs are so powerful that they can transform our physical state? Unfortunately, though, the placebo effect also works in reverse. If you believe a medication has harmful side effects, then you are more likely to experience those effects. People might say 'it is all in the mind', but in fact, the experiences we have every single day are all in our beliefs.

Remember, just like placebos, the beliefs that are shaping your life do not need to be true. If you genuinely believe that red underpants give you more energy, then on a day you feel weary, you are more likely to choose to wear them. If you truly believe in the existence of a higher power, then on the days you are struggling, you are more likely to call on support and assistance from your deity. If you truly believe that you are not beautiful, then you will either attempt to transform into your ideal or hide away from the world out of fear and shame.

Beliefs Are Self-Fulfilling Prophecies

Beliefs are the single most powerful predictor of how you have experienced your life in the past and how you will experience your life in the future. You may have taken action in the past by changing your behaviour—for example, by dieting or exercise. Still, these actions were done to create, change or reinforce beliefs about yourself. We have seen how the mindset you have around your beauty influences your choices, behaviour, perceptions and personality. So it is no surprise that if you believe you are not beautiful, you never will be. This belief has an impact on how you perceive the events that unfold around you. You are more likely to use insults or criticism to reinforce this belief, rather than just see it as the transitory opinion of others. You will shy away from opportunities that can help you to grow, bloom and share your gifts with the world. Hiding away only works to reinforce your belief that you are not beautiful.

However, if you believe that you deserve to be happy and already are beautiful, you will keep yourself healthy and surround yourself with supportive networks. Eating well, doing movement you love, spending time with positive people and practising nourishing rituals will reinforce your personal power. They will accentuate your incredible beauty and help you feel expressed in this world. The belief that you deserve to be happy has created the result that in fact, you are happy. But do not just take my word for it. Here are the experiences of many wise teachers:

'One life is all we have, and we live it as we believe in living it.
But to sacrifice what you are and to live without belief,
that is a fate more terrible than dying.'
~ Joan of Arc

'If you believe you can, you probably can. If you believe you won't,
you most assuredly won't. Belief is the ignition switch that gets
you off the launching pad.'
~ Denis Waitley

'Beliefs have the power to create and the power to destroy.'
~ Tony Robbins

'The outer conditions of a person's life will always be found to reflect their inner beliefs'
~ James Allen

'If I believe I cannot do something, it makes me incapable of doing it. When I believe I can, I acquire the ability to do it even if I didn't have it in the beginning.'
~ Mahatma Gandhi

'The world we see that seems so insane is the result of a belief system that is not working. To perceive the world differently, we must be willing to change our belief system, let the past slip away, expand our sense of now and dissolve the fear in our minds.'
~ William James

Confronting Your Beliefs is an Act of Courage

'You can choose courage, or you can choose comfort.
You cannot have both.'

~ Brené Brown

The Levels of Consciousness shows us that if we want to move to a place of appreciation and to a life of self-love, then we need courage. This courage is required in enormous amounts to investigate and challenge our beliefs. This is because for those beliefs that are embedded, they have become part of our identity. Observing and challenging the beliefs we hold is, therefore, a process of observing and questioning how we view ourselves and how we operate in this world.

Realistically, it is so much easier just to stay in our current patterns and follow the crowd. But is staying in the place that you are now really where you want to be? Acknowledging and accepting your beliefs and how they are shaping your reality takes great courage. When this bravery is combined with the discipline and effort to make personal changes in your life, it is true heroism.

Some of the beliefs you may uncover about yourself may be uncomfortable. However, with knowledge of them comes the power to change them. You can liken the experience to beginning a new exercise routine. At the start, it is challenging. There are physical aches and pains and mental resistance. But this does not detract from the positive impacts of being fit and healthy. Or what about the discipline required to learn a musical instrument? Day after day, week after week, you practise playing your instrument for the end goal of being able to express yourself through music. It is the act of accepting, not resisting, this discomfort that will allow you to move towards the person you can truly become.

With these examples, though, the results are relatively predictable. The difference with exploring your beliefs is that the consequences are unknown. Confronting the reality of our beliefs is a step into uncertainty. It is the fear of the unknown that may be your greatest challenge on this journey. While your current situation may create much distress, it can be viewed as a safe little space because we know what to expect. Have you ever heard of the phrase, 'Better the devil you know'? This saying is used to convince people to stay in their current situations as moving somewhere else, into the unknown, could be much worse. Here is the thing, though—even if where you are now it is the devil you know, it is still a devil. Why?

- Because you are spending a precious asset—time—on things that are not bringing you to your best self.

- Because you are spending another precious asset—energy—doing things that are not helping you live to your full potential.

- Because by staying where you are, you are signalling to friends, children and family that comfort is more important to you than taking a stand for your own wellbeing and freedom.

So yes, you may not know what is on the other side of identifying and challenging your beliefs. But if you know right now that you are not living to your full potential, then make no mistake—you are making a choice to stay with this devil and waste your time and energy. Your time and energy, once spent, cannot be retrieved. These are gifts you will not get back.

However, it is just as likely that some of the beliefs that you find may be encouraging and enlightening. Perhaps they had been hidden away while you navigated the expectations of others. Maybe there is an abundance of creativity you had forgotten about, or perhaps there is a wealth of compassion and love within you that is waiting for you. So, if you are ready to go exploring, now is the time to bring these beliefs out into the light and let them help you shine.

By understanding your beliefs and taking action to transform those that do not serve you, you have the power to shape your destiny. It does not matter where you are now, only what direction your beliefs are taking you in. It does not matter what has happened in your past. The only concern is what your beliefs are helping you to become.

The Most Dangerous Belief

There are many beliefs we have that can limit our flourishing. However, I would like to propose that there is one belief that, if embedded in our psyche, is truly devastating. That is the belief that you are not worthy—not worthy of love, not worthy of care and not worthy of letting the true 'you' shine. If you subscribe to the notion that you do not deserve all of the wonderful things in life, then ultimately you would not take action to achieve them. When opportunities come along to fulfil your greatest dreams and desires, they will be ignored, dismissed or self-sabotaged to prevent them from coming to fruition.

It is this deep belief that threatens every element of your blooming. It impacts on the actions you take on your health—what you choose to do and not to do in order to keep your body and mind well. It influences the people you choose to be around and how honestly you interact with them. If someone really believes that they are a 'bad' person or not worthy of happiness, then the choices they make will support that. They will treat their bodies and minds with little or intermittent care, and show sparse concern for the selection of friends or the quality of relationships with them. If a person believes they are not worthy of financial freedom, they will squander their income and rack up debt. If someone believes their true nature is not worthy of being shared with the world, then it will be hidden away.

The other danger is when a person believes their worth is contingent on something else. For example, several women I know feel that they are only worthy of acceptance if they have a partner—if someone else has 'chosen' to be with them. Some other women only consider that they deserve 'nice' food if they have worked out every day that week. For others, a sense of worthiness is only established when they receive praise from a parent, a teacher, a friend or a boss. If there is only one belief you investigate and challenge through the course of this book, please let it be this one.

Look back now on the list of descriptive words you have chosen in Appendix 1 and see if 'unworthy' is one you have chosen. If you have, or even if you sometimes feel this way, then I want you to wrap yourself up in a big hug. This cuts deep and has an intense impact on your whole life. Now is the time, with love and support, that we can begin to move you from this toxic soil and transplant yourself to a place of peace, compassion and care—where you have full permission to bloom.

'You determine your worth. Nobody else can do it.
Whatever worth you give yourself, that shall be.'

~ Yogi Bhajan

How Beliefs Have Shaped Your Current Reality

As we have seen in Chapter 3, becoming the author of your future is about becoming conscious of the way you think and by questioning your attitudes and behaviours. Let us use a series of questions to understand how your beliefs have shaped your current reality. Then let us go further to identify what you would have to believe about yourself in order to live a full and bona fide life.

Reflect on a time that you had a fantastic result. You may have nailed a difficult task at work, had an awkward conversation with someone that went really well or got your personal best score during a sports match or at training. Picture this positive result in your mind and work backwards through the Action Cycle at the beginning of this chapter (Figure 23) and ask yourself the following questions:

- What did I do or not do (behaviours and actions) that led to this result?

- What was I feeling when I was taking (or not taking) this action?

- What thoughts were occurring for me at this time?

- What beliefs was I holding about myself and my abilities that drove these thoughts?

Now, let us try a different scenario. Reflect on a time when something turned out badly for you. You may have been criticised for the quality of your work or hurt by the words or actions of someone you admire. Or despite an enormous amount of training, you didn't achieve your performance goal. Picture this difficult result in your mind. Again, work backwards through the Action Cycle and ask yourself the following questions:

- What did I do or not do that may have contributed to this result?

- What was I feeling when I was taking (or not taking) this action?

- What thoughts were occurring for me at this time?

- What beliefs was I holding about myself and my abilities that drove these thoughts?

There are so many contributing factors to our successes and our lessons that there is not often a clear line of inference. However, let me give you an example that might shed some light on the relationship between results and beliefs. A friend confided in me that she was feeling hopeless after a break-up with her boyfriend. We worked back from the break-up (the result) to make the following revelation. Before the break-up, she had reduced the amount of time she spent with him. She had started choosing to be by herself or hang out with friends than to be with him. Why was this? Investigating her feelings, she admitted to being really uncomfortable and nervous around him.

But what thoughts were fuelling these feelings? She was thinking that he was charming and great at drawing her out of her shell. She thought that he seemed genuine about getting to know the real her. However, he also called her beautiful. This friend struggled with her body image and confidence throughout her life and would always brush off compliments when they were given to her. She really did not believe she was beautiful. She just couldn't see it in herself.

This lack of belief in her own beauty made her incredibly suspicious of this man. Rather than be uplifted by his words, she felt conflicted and mistrusting of his motives. This belief led to actions that sabotaged a relationship that could have fostered her growth and had the potential to create a nurturing space for her to shine.

Luckily for my friend, gaining this insight turned things around for herself. She was ready and willing to take the next step forward in life and brave enough to become the author of her own story. She met with the ex-boyfriend and explained the situation. She revealed what she had learned about her own behaviour and concerns. She even took a huge risk and opened up to him about the difficult feelings that arose when he called her beautiful. The risk, in this case, was worth it. The ex-boyfriend responded with the words 'wow', and 'you are amazing'. While I cannot predict where their relationship may go, they have spent more time together because my friend accepted how her beliefs formed her reality.

But things could have gone very differently. My friend could have opened up and shared her vulnerability and, in return, could have been ridiculed. Her concerns could have been dismissed or, even worse, the ex-boyfriend could have been utterly apathetic to her pain. But my friend knew that his response would speak volumes about his maturity and care for her. In a way, the conversation was a test to see if this could be a relationship that would support her quest to live her best life and to bloom with her beauty. She was quite prepared to walk away but, this time, her courage paid off and she found a great friend to encourage and aid her journey.

WHAT NEXT?

It would have been wonderful if the ex-boyfriend, when hearing my friend's plight, jumped up on the table and began singing, 'You are so worthy.' But this is not the point. Someone else can tell you that you are worthy, amazing, cool, smart, kind, brave, beautiful, but if you do not honestly believe it in your own heart, then they are just words. In the next chapter, we will investigate why it is your opinion about yourself that matters the most. It is how you think and feel about yourself that is ultimately going to determine your destiny to bloom.

COMMITMENT STATEMENT

I commit to confronting my limiting beliefs
with courage and compassion and to challenge
myself any time the belief of unworthiness arises.

CHAPTER SEVEN
Why Your Beliefs Matter Most

Why Beliefs About Ourselves Really Matter

Now you have a good indication of how you think and feel about yourself. You have taken a great leap forward in becoming aware and accepting of where you are right now. 'But why does doing this matter?' I hear you ask. If the aim is to bloom and grow, why is the view you have of yourself now important? The way you see yourself now is critical to your path forward because it is the driver of action.

You have a list of thoughts and feelings about yourself, some of which make you feel energetic and optimistic, whereas others make you feel drained and inferior. It is these beliefs, thoughts and feelings that have created the actions you have taken up until this very moment, and which have you now reading my love filled words written for you. Your helpful beliefs, thoughts and feelings have led to moments of learning and growth. Your problematic beliefs, thoughts and emotions have led to behaviours and outcomes that have limited or depleted your physical and mental wellbeing and your sense of self-worth. Going back to the previous chapter with the Self-Fulfilling Action Cycle from beliefs to results, can you see how the cycle works? Let's take an example:

- Belief—say you believe that you look ugly in a swimsuit. You have looked at yourself in the mirror wearing the latest style and feel embarrassed.

- Thoughts—when you receive an invitation to go to the beach with friends, you immediately think that you won't swim because people will judge you and make fun of you.

- Feelings—the thought of sitting on the beach makes you feel sad. You love the feel of the water and the freedom of diving through the waves. You love the sensation of the sun on your skin and the ocean breeze on your body. Knowing that you won't be doing this brings a state of despair.

- Behaviour—you go to the beach with friends and spend the time covered in a baggy shirt and shorts. You sit on the sand, watching everyone else swim.

- Results—perhaps you hear others criticising another girl about her figure and feel relieved that you didn't show your body in your swimmers too. Your friends are so thankful that you were there to mind their bags. You feel comfortable with your choice, but aware of how much joy you have missed.

- Confirmed belief—the thoughts, feelings and actions you have taken have confirmed for you that being seen in your swimmers is too risky. It has reinforced your belief that your body is a problem that must be 'fixed' if you do want to go swimming in the ocean.

So the cycle continues, and you spend each day wishing you were brave enough not to care about what your body looks like and that you could just enjoy your days while you have them.

What you believe, think and feel about yourself and others has, in this case, caused behaviours that have compromised your enjoyment of life. You have withheld your best, joyous self because of these thoughts and feelings. So I'm going to lovingly remind you that the views you have of yourself are incredibly important because they will determine your actions.

Negative beliefs about yourself or a prioritised concern about the opinions of others can result in taking actions that limit your own enjoyment and sacrifice your own happiness. It stunts your growth and prevents you from being able to bloom and share your unique and beautiful gifts with the world. So where does this preoccupation with the negative beliefs of ourselves and others come from? Why does it have so much influence over our lives?

A Basic Human Need

There are very few things that, as humans, we really need to survive. One of these, however, is the need to feel good about ourselves. People are intrinsically motivated to take actions that will enhance their sense of self-worth. It seems to be stating the obvious that people want to feel proud of themselves, not ashamed. They want to feel accepted, not shunned. People want to feel hope and not fear. Boosting our sense of self-worth helps us to manage our fears and worries about living in this world—about being accepted and cared for.

Securing our sense of self-worth is a behaviour that was formed from childhood when we were incredibly vulnerable and dependent on the goodwill and care of adults for our survival. If we could feel good about ourselves, then we were more assured of protection and therefore more likely to survive. But, when we move to adulthood, these behaviours do not just disappear. The need to have a sense of self-worth remains and, unfortunately, so does the tendency to equate this self-worth with the opinions of others. This is normal in the Socialised Mind stage of adult development.

At the End of Your Life, Your Own Opinion Matters Most

It is a sad reality that we often only get to appreciate what is truly important in life when we are nearing its end. While it is heartbreaking, the regrets of those who are dying provide great wisdom for us now. They provide us with knowledge about what we can do to make sure we do not end up dying with regrets. Thanks to Bronnie Ware, a palliative care nurse, we can predict precisely what those regrets will be. Patients that only had weeks to live were asked what their major life regrets were and what they would do differently if they were given a second chance at life. Here are the top five regrets:

1. I wish I pursued my dreams and aspirations and not the life others expected of me;

2. I wish I did not work so hard;

3. I wish I dared to express my feelings and speak my mind;

4. I wish I had stayed in touch with my friends; and

5. I wish I had let myself be happier.

The most common regret among the dying was that they didn't dare to live their own dreams and instead followed the directions and expectations of others. One of the patients, a lady called Grace, made Bronnie promise that she would not hesitate to pursue all her dreams and not give a damn about what anyone else might say. You see, what haunts us in our dying days is not the voices of the critics, but our own dreams and potential that have gone unfulfilled.

The experience of dying patients shows that choosing peace over confrontation stunts your ability to move forward, so the message is clear, take responsibility for your future and live up to your full potential. Honesty and constructive confrontation are part of healthy relationships, and when done with respect and care can improve the connection within the relationships. Expressing our true feelings empowers us in the moment and prevents regrets in the future.

It was only when the patients were at the end of their lives that they realised they had the choice all along to be happy. Like so many of us, they had spent their lives chasing happiness through possessions or the acceptance of others. In their dying days, they gained the wisdom that they had the choice to be happy, regardless of what their circumstances were. They realised that it was not the 'things' that created happiness; it was their own minds and hearts all along. Being here, alive, you still have time.

I say that with awareness comes responsibility. Now that you know what motivates the judgements of others and have heard the voices of those dying with regrets, you have a choice. Who do you listen to? Do you listen to:

- The judgements of others, which are formed purely from their understandings and needs?

- Your own heart, which is who you must rest with at the end of each day?

- The regrets of those who are dying, who can look back and see what is truly important?

What Do You Want to be Known For?

'I've learned that people will forget what you said, people will forget what you did, but people will never forget how you made them feel.'

~ Maya Angelou

You have so many wonderful qualities that should be celebrated. Some may be acknowledged by others, but what matters are the qualities and characteristics that are meaningful for you. To help you determine what these are—what you value and hold dear—here are some critical questions.

Project yourself into the future. Imagine yourself ten years from now, and you are about to speak about your incredible journey of self-discovery and growth. A host is introducing you to the crowd. What are the characteristics and qualities you have shown that you want the host to mention in their introduction? Refer to the list in Appendix 1 for some guidance. Write down all the things you want to be known for and then looking at the list, highlight those you have already chosen to describe yourself now.

- Are there any new characteristics that have shown up?

- What does this tell you about what blooming might look like for you?

- How many of the things you have written down are physical characteristics and how many are internal qualities?

- What does this say about what is truly important for you at this time?

WHAT NEXT?

We have journeyed into the thoughts and feelings you have about yourself now and begun to shine a light on what is important for you in the future. But sometimes the beliefs we may need to challenge are deeply rooted in traumatic or significant events from our past. Sometimes the shadows cast by the past appear bigger than us and threaten to keep us in the dark and cold. So how do we move forward when we are bound by the embarrassments or shames of the past? How can we find the courage to bloom when we are constantly reminded of their harmful history?

Ultimately it is your choice about how much of your history goes into your future. There is only one certainty: you are not going to get where you want to go and finally make peace with your body if you continue to do the things you have always done. So let us find out how to remove the shackles of the past so that you can move forward with courage and compassion.

COMMITMENT STATEMENT

I commit to living a life with no regrets and taking responsibility to let my unique beauty shine.

CHAPTER EIGHT
Making Peace with the Past

'Sometimes, you just have to make peace with your past
to keep your future from becoming a constant battle.'
~ Susan Gale

Sometimes it is not the things that we are experiencing in the present moment that hold us back from being our best. Sometimes we are clinging on to actions and events from the past that are limiting the beliefs we have about ourselves and are keeping us stuck in patterns of self-sabotaging behaviour. Sure, the past has *shaped* who we are right now. But the stories of the past do not have to *define* who we are. These stories show that we are human. So before we can move forward, we may need to acknowledge and heal the things from our past that are weighing us down in the lower levels of consciousness, such as shame, fear, anger or guilt.

On close inspection, feelings that are life-destroying and reside in the category of force are grounded in the past. Guilt and shame are derived from things we have done that have been against social norms or against our own moral standards. Pride comes from hanging onto past achievements, and anger is fuelled from prior events where our needs and wants were not met. Even desire is driven by an urge to relive past experiences that have provided pleasure.

It seems ludicrous though it is a very normal action for many, that we allow events from the past to have so much influence over our lives now. Every new moment is precious, and with every breath, we can start anew. So why is it that so many of us choose to hang onto past hurts? Why do we continue to beat ourselves up with thoughts and feelings that hold us in a pattern of self-sabotage? These lower-level thoughts and feelings keep you in the past and inhibit your innate ability to move forward and bloom.

The higher levels of consciousness move from a focus on the past to concern and care for the future. We have discussed the principal gateway of courage previously, and this is the feeling and action that helps you begin to see life as exciting rather than draining. With courage, you know the potential for improving on the past, rather than continuing to dwell within it. At the point of acceptance, you recognise and respect your incredible potential, and take proactive action to shine your potential in all that you do.

It is just so easy to say it's not for me. But when you are buried deep in anger, fear, grief or guilt, the pain is real and the burden is debilitating. How do you begin to shift this negative force? How do you get the courage to peek your head out and embrace the sunshine of potential? How do you leave behind the heartache of the past and move onwards and upwards? There are three steps, all of which call on the remarkable courage that has got you here:

1. Recognition—of the role the past had played.
2. Regret—moving away from guilt and towards regret.

3. Responsibility—moving from blaming others to taking personal responcibility.

Recognition

'You are the sky. Everything else is just the weather.'
~ Pema Chodron

As we read in Chapter 3, the lower levels of consciousness—the limiting states of fear, anger, grief, guilt and shame—are necessary. They do not represent failure. They do not define who you are. All of these feelings are essential. Just think about it for a moment. You did not learn to walk without many tumbles. You cannot be a master pianist without knowing the wrong notes. As agonising as it is, you cannot understand who you truly are without first experiencing all levels of consciousness.

Every time we experience one of the distressing emotions, inherently, we are also learning about its opposite. Grief teaches us about the nature of love, shame teaches us about self-acceptance, anger shows us the blessing of peace and pride can lead us to feel joy. So, all of your experiences have led you closer to understanding all the levels of consciousness. They all have acted as gates on the path of your blooming. But they do not define you, and they are certainly not who you are. They are not your legacy. They are simply your understanding. What defines you is what you do next with what you have learned.

I could go one step further and suggest that all of your past experiences should actually be celebrated or thanked. All the falls, all the wrong notes, all the twists and turns of your life have brought you here—reading this book. Without them, you would not be at this point of self-awareness. You would not have the courage to dig deep to find the real and beautiful you. You would not have the understanding that you are much greater than any single one of these experiences.

Regret

When was the last time you felt guilty about something? Picture the situation in your mind. How does being guilty for something make you feel? More than likely, it would come with a severe dose of shame or anger and self-hatred. You may be feeling a little stupid and berating your lack of skill, morality and judgement.

But can you see what is happening here with guilt? With guilt comes an exaggerated sense of responsibility for the situation. You end up taking full liability, which is unrealistic and unfair. We act as our own judge and jury and declare that we were wholly and solely at fault and therefore are obviously a horrendous person. How could any good come from such an act of self-scourging?

Well, like any emotion, guilt sends us a message that something is not quite right. It is a beacon that shows us we have acted outside our moral boundaries and against our values. Guilt is a sign that we have hurt a value or person we hold dear. In this way, when we feel guilt arising, we can use it as a prompt that some reflection on our actions would be useful. However, it is just so tempting to use the feeling of guilt to dramatise our activities and to reinforce our limiting self-beliefs.

When this happens, guilt becomes a weapon for self-harm and self-sabotage. It harms us because it fosters a negative view of ourselves and our abilities. It sabotages our future because this narrow and harsh view of ourselves makes it very difficult to move forward in any proactive and positive way. We get so caught up in our mistakes that we cannot see the role others played in the situation and direct all the guilt towards ourselves. There is no doubt that for some, guilt is a feeling and behaviour expected by others as part of the process of apology. Sometimes, we also expect it from ourselves as the way we must display contrition for our regrets.

The reality is, though, apart from the spark of self-awareness it provides, there is absolutely no other benefit of guilt. It will keep you stuck in childish behaviours and limiting beliefs. There is a much healthier, positive approach, and that is regret. Regret is a mature response because rather than wallowing in self-pity, it seeks to learn from a situation and move on to a better state of being. While guilt closes hearts and minds, regret opens them to the opportunities for healing. It creates the potential for restoration with ourselves and others.

To move away from guilt and to achieve the benefits that regret can bring, work through the following:

- Get real with the hardship and hurt. The aim of regret is to learn from our mistakes. We can only do this if we are honest about the amount of hurt that our actions have caused, not only for others but also for ourselves. If you really do not believe that the consequences of your actions are significant, then there is not much encouragement to prevent the behaviour again in the future. This requires courage and to think deeply and honestly about the troubles that your actions have caused. This reflection is not pretty, but it is only by working through the dirt and the mud that we can find the sun and bloom.

- Make a resolution. Once you have a full appreciation of the regret, you can move forward and make a promise—a decision not to make the same regret again. If your resolution feels slightly superficial or weak, then this is because not enough time and energy has been spent on getting real with it. If the outcomes of the actions hold little significance for you, then there will be very little motivation behind your resolution. It will be driven from a position of force, something you feel obliged to do, instead of being an action born from acceptance and love.

- Take remedial action. After all the contemplation is complete, it is time to take action to restore what is important to you. The most important relationship is the one that you have with yourself, and it is the first one you need to work on to recover and fully heal from a regret. We hold such high expectations of ourselves and are more critical of ourselves than our worst enemy. While we can forgive others, sometimes it is much more difficult to forgive ourselves. Seeking forgiveness and repairing is essential to healing past mistakes. However, forgiving ourselves and loving ourselves through the process of learning and growing is the bravest thing you will ever do.

There is always the risk that if your regret hurts someone else in the process, they may not be ready to forgive and may want to hold onto the pain. This could happen if they operate from the lower levels of consciousness and act out of pride and fear. Perhaps they are enjoying abdicating responsibility for their own lives and blaming you for their situation. There is nothing you can do about this. You are only responsible for your own actions, and not for other people's reactions. If you have spent some time first with yourself—understanding, and forgiving yourself—then you can learn and grow from whatever the response of others may be.

Responsibility

'You can fail many times, but you are not a failure
until you begin to blame somebody else.'
~ John Burroughs

If guilt is the act of exaggerating our part in a situation, then blame is the act of placing full responsibility and accountability onto someone else. I am the first to admit that when something goes wrong, it is just so easy to find a scapegoat. Blame takes the focus off me and, for a moment, I can live in the delusion that someone else is entirely the cause of my despair. How wonderful it is not to have to invest any time or energy in self-reflection or personal development.

Right then and there, with blame, we have placed fault on someone else and secured our attachment to the past. We have narrowed our focus to those things that other people should have done or said, and we have created hearts that are closed. Blame is sinister, and while it may feel good for a moment, this relief soon passes. Blame leaves you feeling separated from others, discontent and closed off from your own creativity and hope for the future.

The opposite path to blame is responsibility. This involves looking at the whole situation, being aware of the role that you have played in the outcome. For example, blame shows up as anger at a friend who came to visit and made you miss your gym class. Instead, responsibility sees that you created your own stress by allocating insufficient time for the catch-up or not setting a clear boundary. Blame accuses your partner for your poor eating habits as they always cook greasy food. In contrast, responsibility admits that you always can make dinner for yourself. Blame looks to your children or your work commitments for your poor physical fitness. In comparison, responsibility understands that you are in control of your health and how you use your time.

As long as we spend our time searching for someone else to hold responsible, our mind will never be at peace. Our precious time will be wasted away, looking for a target for our anger and discontent. Would your time and energy not be better spent on the work required to reach your full potential? Would it not be better invested in making you grow and bloom, rather than to keep other people oppressed? When you think about it, spending your precious assets on resentment and blame is incredibly selfish. You are choosing to use your energy on things that tie you to the past, rather than those that will help you be the best person you can be in the future. You are sacrificing your true potential, which will help make this world a better place for you, your family and for generations to come.

If you really are ready to bloom and grow, then you need to take responsibility for your behaviour and your situation. To move forward, you have to stop the search for scapegoats, stop blaming the world, stop living in the past and start opening your heart and mind to the bigger picture of your potential. There is no doubt about it—taking responsibility is tough, confronting and painful. It is not pretty. There is no 'glamping' option on the path to your self-discovery. But getting real with yourself and taking accountability for your current situation will liberate you and put you on the way to your full blooming.

Silver Linings

One way to help process difficult times from the past is also to look at them through the lens of silver linings. Each and every event in our lives—ones we see as good, and those we see as bad—all have the potential to teach us valuable lessons and bring us home to our own unique beauty. Here is how the process of silver linings works.

Think about a difficult time from the past. One that felt overwhelming and impossible to get through. Yet, here you are, still standing and ready to tell the tale. While there may have been much pain and distress, there is always another side of the coin. With the gift of hindsight, think about what the silver linings of this experience were. Here are some questions that may help:

- What did I learn about myself?

- What did I learn about the way the world works?

- What did I learn about other people?

- What would I have missed out on if this experience did not occur?

- What would I do differently next time?

- What would I do the same next time?

Here is an example from a client who went through a prolonged and challenging bullying situation at university due to her large breasts. She was considering having breast reduction surgery. She very wisely sought me out to help her rebuild her confidence and find some silver linings with her experience. These are some of her insights:

What did I learn about myself?

- That under stress, I do tend to stop doing things that are important to stay well. For example, eating well, sleeping and exercising.

- I am much stronger than I think.

- I have a colossal trigger when I feel like I am being singled out for attention.

- Kindness and compassion are really important values for me.

What did I learn about how the world works?

- There is no-one else that is going to take responsibility for your health and wellbeing—it is all up to you!

- Society's definition of beauty is a really restricted one—there is not much room to be different.

- It does help to get an independent opinion about how to deal with an issue.

What did I learn about other people?

- Some people find my body threatening.

- Some people take their insecurities and fears out on other people.

- Some people actually go out of their way to hurt others.

What would I have missed out on if this experience did not occur?

- The chance to get stronger and more courageous around how I relate to my body.

- The opportunity of learning all about what drives bullying behaviour.

- The motivation to start my own blog to help other girls in the same situation and to find my own tribe.

- The chance to really care for and appreciate my body, big breasts and all!

What would I do differently next time?

- I would take better care of my physical and mental health throughout the process.

- I would journal about my experience to have something to help others in the same situation.

- Know that I am perfect just as I am and should not be ashamed of my traits.

What would I do the same next time?

- I would not give up—I have gained so much courage from the process.

- I would use the experience to realise I do not belong in every peer group.

- I would use the experience to seek out my own place in this world, rather than rely on other people to do this for me.

Look at all of the incredible learnings that came from that one event. It is easy to hold onto bitterness and blame, but this silver linings exercise helps you take responsibility for finding positive outcomes in all of your life experiences.

Now, think of a challenge or a struggle that you are currently going through. Is there any problem that is keeping you up at night and seems really difficult to resolve? Maybe it is something about your body or features that are really getting you down. You have likely been so caught up in the experience that you have not had a chance to take a fresh perspective and look for the silver linings. Take a few moments now to imagine:

- What positive outcomes could come from this experience?

- How could you learn and grow from this situation?

Each and every one of your past experiences has delivered invaluable blessings. Have faith that no matter how hard your current situation may feel, this time will be no different.

'If you change the way you look at things,
the things you look at change.'
~ Dr Wayne Dyer

WHAT NEXT?

I hope that this chapter has confirmed that your past does not define you. If you can bring consciousness and care to past events, you can learn and grow from them. You can use them to find the motivation and power to move forward. Yes, your past shapes you, but it is not you. It prepares you for what you are becoming. Remember the Levels of Consciousness model? This model makes it clear that you have to work through the lower levels to be able to arrive at a place of courage, love and joy. Your history has helped you move through these painful levels so that you can now move towards becoming the very best version of you.

'You are not your past. Although you are changed and shaped by past experiences, who you were yesterday does not control the person you have the potential to become tomorrow.'

~ Sue Augustine

In the next chapter, we will go even deeper. We will rediscover the beauty and power that exists already within you. Let's take one more step into retreat and meet the perfect seed.

COMMITMENT STATEMENT

I commit to not letting my past hurts dictate my future, but commit to using them as preparation for my incredible future.

CHAPTER NINE
The Seed is Perfect

So far, we have spent our time considering different views and opinions about beauty. But what do we have in the way of facts? What can we find that can inform our understanding of beauty and which cannot be refuted? For this, we only have to look into the natural world. There are realities we see unfolding in nature every single day that are not tainted by what anyone thinks or says; they are just real and genuine. There is no better place to witness this truth than in a seed.

It does not matter whether it is a tiny mustard seed or as big as a coconut; the seed has everything it needs to fulfil its destiny. It holds a remarkable intelligence and knowledge that does not depend on anything else but the right environment for it to reach its full potential. The seed knows what it is meant to become, and how to become it. It knows whether it is intended to become an orchid or an oak tree, and it knows the steps it needs to take to get there.

On the outside, the seed may appear incredibly uninspiring. It may be a dull brown bead or a tiny black speck. But this dry hard coat holds an embryo of a complete plant—roots, shoots and all. It contains enough food to sustain it until it has developed roots and leaves to take in nutrients from the soil and sun. When we hold a seed in our hands, it may look lifeless. But in fact, it is just dormant. It is waiting until it is in the right environment to germinate. In the right conditions, the seed will spring to life, shoot out of its protective home and rise up into the world.

We can stand above the seed every day and tell it to become a tomato plant, but it will grow into what it is meant to be. We can say to the seed every day that it is ugly and that it does not fit in with the other plants, but it will grow anyway. We can tell the seed that no-one likes its fruit or flowers, that it is wasting time growing. Yet, it will grow anyway. It is intent on delivering on the promise to share its gifts with the world. Labels we place on the seed are meaningless. It is only the nature of the seed that truly counts.

However, you do not always know what seed you have until you give it a chance to grow. When we buy seeds from a store, we are lucky to have them labelled, so we know what to expect. But what happens if you plant one and have no idea what type of seed it is? Then you have the most excellent adventure before you. A future that cannot be predicted, and yet one that you know, with the right care, will bring many gifts.

So, it only stands to reason that the process we see for the seed also holds true for us. As human beings, we are made of the same natural processes. Just as a seed is created from a fertilised mature ovule, so it was in our own beginning. However, we have even more than the little seed. We have the ability for self-reflection, questioning, learning and change within our lifetimes. We can forge new pathways in our brain, develop new habits and skills, and cease those that are not serving us. So, while we have grown physically, it is only in our own hearts that we know whether we have fully bloomed. Only we truly know how much potential remains to share with the world. My hope is that I will help you uncover your true potential and break free to bloom yourself into your world—which you know has already begun.

There is one more observation I must make, and one more question I must ask. When we plant seeds, there is such excitement when we see the first green shoots of a new plant. We watch, care for and cheer on the new little plant every step of the way. So, why is it that we can do this for a seed, but we find this so hard to do for ourselves? Why is it that we can play the role of tender gardener for life outside of ourselves, and yet take on the role of harsh critic for the life that shines in our own hearts? We nurture the seeds of plants by finding the right soil and protecting it from predators, as well as watering, feeding and celebrating its growth. Yet, we allow our internal seeds, our unique potential, to be trampled by others and sprayed with toxic opinions. We even ignore and neglect the nutritional needs of our own seeds.

There are many reasons we care for others much more than ourselves, and we will unpack many of these throughout these pages. Knowing a seed has all the knowledge it needs to grow. So, do you. You have all the wisdom you will ever need right within you. It is now a process of creating the right environment for you to connect with your beautiful miracle and to allow your potential to bloom.

You Are Perfect

'Seeds never lose their potential, not even in the dirt.'
~ Matshona Dhliwayo

When I say these words—you are perfect—I can imagine what your reaction could be. Perhaps you respond dismissively with, 'You are full of it.' Maybe you say a polite 'thank you' but brush it aside. Or perhaps you let it sink in and reaffirm what you truly believe about yourself. Naturally, I was prone to respond in one of the first two ways. My mind would turn instantly to my critical points—the shortcomings I've been given and made, and all of the hurt I have given and received. A montage of painful memories comes flooding in and provides evidence that I am far from perfect. It is understandable if you choose to use these past experiences to reinforce your negative self-belief—to stay in your little seed and not try to break out and bloom. This behaviour does not make you deficient. It makes you completely normal. Most people are unsatisfied with their lives, but just keep doing what they have always done. Why should you be any different?

But even if you do not believe it yet, I believe that you are perfect, and I believe it with all of my heart and my soul. I am here to help you believe it for yourself, because acknowledging and loving how unique and special you are is at the heart of forging your own path. It is the foundation of finally being able to bloom and to love being you.

I know we are taught to be modest and not to boast about our own abilities. Nobody likes to be around someone who appears arrogant and overconfident. We are very good at cutting down tall poppies to a size that makes us feel more comfortable about ourselves. However, humility is not a quality that should just be reserved for display to others. It is a quality that will keep us seeking more, learning more and continually growing to be the best person we can be. But without acknowledging the innate perfection, truth and wisdom within you, it is difficult to move forward with excitement and trust. If you can't commit to the notion of your perfection yet, suspend your disbelief and entertain the possibility that within yourself resides a wisdom that you have only begun to witness.

Perhaps to help you along, some evidence of your awesomeness would be of assistance? Here are some facts that might help:

- You are unique. There is no-one else on the planet with your genetic makeup, your fingerprints and your perspective. There is only one you. For this precise reason, it does not make any sense to compare yourself to anyone else. No-one else thinks exactly like you do, and no-one else can make the exact difference you can make in this world. You cannot change this world by being like it, so it is time to not only accept your unique perfection but to embrace it.

- You are reading this book. I know this is an obvious statement, but the fact that you are here now reading this book is incredibly important. It shows that you are not satisfied with the status quo and that you are willing to invest your time and energy to live up to your true potential. It shows that you are:

  ◊ Brave—you dare to challenge your beliefs and behaviours and strive to be the best you can be. It also takes a lot of guts to take responsibility for your future, but here you are, doing exactly that.

  ◊ Wise—you are seeking knowledge and know-how to find the help you need. Seeking help shows that you do have a deep faith in yourself and your ability to reach your potential.

  ◊ Resilient—there is no doubt, you have experienced the many ups and downs of life. Yet, here you are. You have survived, you have dressed your wounds and cared for your scars, and now you are ready to take on the next great challenge.

- You see and appreciate beauty. Take a quick look around you right now. Can you find something that you would class as beautiful? Can you find something that inspires you? It could be the sky, a flower, an impressive building or a carefully prepared meal. Whatever it may be, the fact that you see this beauty in something outside of yourself means that it resides within you. You cannot appreciate beauty if it is not something that is already embedded in your nature.

'Though we travel the world over to find the beautiful,
we must carry it with us, or we find it not.'
~ Ralph Waldo Emerson

If there is only one thing you take away from this chapter, let it be this: blooming is not a process of 'fixing' yourself. It is not a process of relearning to love yourself and knowing that your body is beautiful, it always has been. It is the understanding that there was nothing wrong with you to begin with. You are perfect, whole and worthy, just as you are.

'Drop the idea of becoming someone because you are
already a masterpiece. You cannot be improved.
You have only to come to it, to know it, to realise it.'
~ Osho

What Do You Think?

You have read my beliefs about how amazing you already are. Now I would like to hear what you think. Coco Chanel once said: 'Beauty begins the moment you decide to be yourself.'

Consider this statement and contemplate the following questions:

- Do you believe this statement holds true for the people you love and care for? For example, friends, family and children? Why or why not?

- Do you believe this statement holds true for you? Why or why not?

Now think about my assertion that you are perfect, whole and worthy, just as you are. Ask yourself the same questions about this statement:

- Do you believe this statement holds true for the people you love and admire? Why or why not?

- Do you believe this statement holds true for you? Why or why not?

WHAT NEXT?

Congratulations! You have reached the end of The Retreat.

In the next chapter, we will reflect on how far you have come to an understanding of your body, your beliefs and your unique spirit.

COMMITMENT STATEMENT

I commit to acknowledging and appreciating
the perfect seed within and caring for my
amazing potential every day.

CHAPTER TEN

Reflection on The Retreat

'Within you, there is a stillness and a sanctuary to which
you can retreat at any time and be yourself.'
~ Hermann Hesse

The Purpose of The Retreat

For many of us, our days are spent chasing happiness in all manner of ways. What we do every day is a balancing act between avoiding discomfort and achieving pleasure. We act from fear of the disapproval of friends, family and peers. We strive to create a life we love, where we can feel free and at peace. But around our personal dreams and desires, there is a whole world of noise and pollution. Our journeys are hampered by the constant barrage of our own and other people's expectations. We are faced every day with a cacophony of conflicting messages telling us what is beautiful, what is not, what your body should look like, what it should not and how to 'fix' it.

Navigating your way through this world to find a place that is true to the unique and beautiful you is incredibly difficult. Yet we only have to look to the people we admire for their authenticity to know that it is possible. The journey through requires great focus, courage and effort, and that is why The Retreat is so important. A retreat is a place where you strip away the noise, listen to your heart and come to a place of understanding. It is to create a space of stillness and silence, where you can tap into your inherent wisdom and reconnect with the perfect seed within. A retreat brings you back to your home for shelter and supports you until you are ready to head out again on the great adventure of blooming and sharing your beauty with this world.

If you are coming to this book weary and scarred from battles with your body and spirit, then the wisest thing to do is to retreat. To take some time, restore your energy and set the direction for the next move forward. If you were on a battlefield, heavily outnumbered and headed for defeat, would you stay and keep fighting? Of course not! To protect your troops and your ability to win the war, you would retreat to a safe place where you can gather your strength. You would take time to reflect on what you have learned about the enemy and yourself in order to plan the next best move.

The key difference with your life, though, is that it is not a matter of winning a war. The ultimate goal is to win yourself—your real and beautiful self. Winning is giving yourself permission to be the wonderful and exceptional you. It is being able to love your body and to bloom into your unique beauty that has always resided inside of you.

The Role of Your Body

Coming to accept and care for your body is first a process of acknowledging the role that it plays in your life. While yes, your physical form is an important tool to interact with others—it is so much more than that. It is also the home for your spirit, your soul and your incredible potential. An unbalanced focus on the external-facing role of your body impedes your confidence to move freely in this world. This is because our actions are not built on a strong foundation of care and respect for the beauty within. When you recognise and come to know the perfect seed within, then the body becomes an expression of this. Treating our bodies only as a façade for the acceptance or appreciation of others puts our sense of worth at great risk and distracts the very limited and precious time and energy we are given each day.

So, on this retreat, the first thing we have done is to recognise that our bodies are much more than a shell for our ego and relationships. Our bodies are the home in which our spirit can be cherished and the seed can be nourished to grow. This retreat has asked you to reflect on which role of the body your priority has been lately, and whether there are any changes you would like to make in this allocation of care. What do you think about your current priorities? How have they been working for you? Do you think your priorities should change in any way and, most importantly, why? Why is your desired split of priorities important to you?

Who Decides What is Physical Beauty?

As you will have become aware, if you do not make considered and conscious decisions for yourself, others are more than willing to do this for you. You have opinions coming from your family, friends and peers. You are surrounded every moment with images from the media, who are always looking for the next new thing to sell. The media largely plays their games at the lower levels of consciousness, working on your guilt, shame, fear, desire and pride in order to get you on board and to sell you stuff.

We have seen just how fickle beauty standards can be, as there has been a roller-coaster of ideal weight and body shapes preferred over time. Before the media, the work of artists celebrated natural female forms. With newspapers and print media came the advertisements for corsets and 'waist training', to create or accentuate the maternal figure. With magazines and television came dieting and exercise fads, along with an escalation of eating disorders.

It is as though we have handed over our individual power to the media to decide what we should look like, and who we should be. How much do you feel like you are influenced by the people you 'follow' or the advertisements you see? Could it be that part of the battle you are in now is between what others tell you is beautiful, and what your body is in all of its natural splendour? Could it be that you have handed over your power by allowing others to define what beauty is for you? Could it be that you are focusing your energy on what you should be now, rather than what you are in the process of becoming and always have been?

Preoccupation with the Physical

We know now that preoccupation with the physical form makes it incredibly difficult to move up the levels of consciousness to happy and productive states such as acceptance and love. Being stuck in the Socialised Mind means that we are beholden to the opinions of others and a slave to meeting their expectations of us. By concentrating on the physical, our days are spent focusing on how we 'fit in', and not on how we can stand out and make our amazing difference in this world.

Breaking Free

But how do we break free from the chains of conformity and begin to feel comfortable in our own skin? This is a process of consciousness and courage. Consciousness is about becoming aware of the beliefs we hold and how they are or are not serving us at this time. So many of our thoughts, feelings and actions are driven by motivations that we are not fully aware of. In fact, your subconscious mind is 30,000 times more powerful than your conscious mind. That is why what we genuinely believe becomes our reality, even if we believe we are actively working towards the opposite. The only way we have a chance to counter those beliefs that are hindering us is if we bring them out into the light and see their true nature. The only way we can bloom is if we have the courage to challenge those that limit our potential. Making peace with your body then is a process of conscious living—being clear about what is dear to you and then making a dedicated effort to live your best life and have confidence in being you.

'Be your own kind of beautiful.'
~ Marilyn Monroe

Finding the Courage

The journey to your authentic self, to your blooming, is not an easy one. Just as the seed has to work through the soil, the weather and predators, so you too will have myriad challenges to your blooming. Some will be presented by others as they begin to fear and feel threatened by any changes in you. However, most challenges will arise within yourself as you face what can be destructive beliefs and behavioural patterns that have been ingrained across generations. It takes incredible bravery to break free from the forces acting as shame, guilt and fear and move towards the life-giving light of acceptance and love. This courage rests upon the ability to connect with your own inherent power, that which does and always has lived within you. Courage comes from using your own power, rather than succumbing to the force that others seek to exert upon you.

Process of Enquiry

Living with consciousness and courage is a continual process of self-enquiry. It involves asking yourself:

- What do I think?

- What do I want?

- What are my motivations?

The Retreat is there to provide you with the stillness and silence to hear and appreciate the responses within you.

What If I Do Not Have the Answers?

Sometimes there may not be a response to the questions you ask. It is understandable that for some of us, we have been subservient to the wishes of others for so long that we have lost our voice. That is absolutely okay! It is just fine if you do not know the answers yet. The crucial thing is that you are asking the questions. The most important thing is that you are taking the time to reflect and that you are calling upon your own power to evaluate what is working, and not working, for you at this moment.

All I would suggest in this situation is that you let the questions sit. Let them open your mind and your heart and trust that the answers will come. It could be minutes, days or years, but when the time is right, the insights will arise. The answers do not always come either as voices in your head. They could show up with some advice from a friend, in your dreams, from the people you meet or in the events that happen around you. Be vigilant and be open, because when you begin to use your power, new doors of insight will be opened. I also love to use the counter question of 'But if I did know the answer, what would it be?' Remembering that blooming is a process, and coming back into your own beauty is no different.

Retreat to Yourself

The Retreat does conclude with this section. It is always available to you when you need to step out of the noise and come back to the true you. In this vast, fast-moving and conflicted world as we launch into The Expedition, there will be times that you will need some peace and time to reflect and restore your weary body, mind and spirit. Taking time to come back to what you believe, what you want and to remind yourself of your own incredible resources will serve you well on what is realistically a lifelong journey. Retreat to find yourself so that you can make peace with your body and bloom into your new phase of beauty.

'Constantly then give to thyself this retreat, and renew thyself.'
~ Marcus Aurelius

Here are some reflection questions to put The Retreat into perspective.

- I believe you are perfect, whole and worthy just as you are. What do you think?

- I believe that your process of blooming is not about 'fixing' yourself, because there was nothing wrong with you to begin with. What do you think?

- What do you want your days to be full of?

- What do you want your days to be free of?

- What were your motivations for picking up this book? What were you hoping for?

- What are you seeking in your life?

- What question do you need answered to move forward?

COMMITMENT STATEMENT

I commit to returning to a place of retreat
whenever I need to restore my
consciousness or courage.

PART B

The Expedition –
Letting Your
Beauty Bloom

CHAPTER ELEVEN

The First Step: Acceptance

Self-Esteem Versus Self-Acceptance

We tend to use the term 'self-esteem' to refer to the way that people feel about themselves. People with high self-esteem have a belief that they are good and worthy, and that others view them positively. Low self-esteem is characterised by a neutral or apathetic feeling towards oneself or a belief that we are inadequate or less worthy than others. In extreme cases, people with low self-esteem have feelings of anger, hate or disgust towards themselves. No matter what level of self-esteem a person has, there is one thing in common, which is that the feelings of self-worth come from a comparison with others.

If you think that increasing your self-esteem is the magic pill that will cure all of your problems, then you are not alone. Since the 1970s, there has been a push to increase self-esteem. It is seen by many as the solution to many of our modern-day problems. In 1986, California funded a task force to raise self-esteem, under the belief that it would have positive effects on affected community problems. This project failed to achieve the desired results. So, in 2003 a new task force was established by the American Psychological Association in order to understand the causes and effects of both high and low self-esteem[11].

The researchers in this study found that people with high self-esteem are more successful academically. They are also generally less stressed and less depressed, and they tend to have longer lives than those with lower levels of self-esteem. But what I believe is the greatest difference between those who had high and low levels of self-esteem is the amount of action that they took. The researchers found that those people who had higher self-esteem were taking more initiative, more action, and generally just did more things. Furthermore, the researchers found that self-esteem in itself was not the driver of this action, but instead the result. This was confirmed when initiatives were undertaken to boost students' self-esteem by telling them how great they were. There was no positive change in their academic performance from this at all.

In fact, a singular focus on self-esteem, having the prime goal to feel good about yourself, is actually diminishing because:

- Concentrating on protecting and enhancing your self-esteem creates stress and anxiety, largely due to concerns about not living up to an ideal. For example, if your self-esteem is linked to academic performance, there will be greater stress leading up to exams due to the worry about performance and the impact on self-worth.

- Seeking to maintain your self-esteem means that you are more likely to follow the views of others. This stunts your ability to act independently, autonomously and for your own best interests.

- The pursuit of self-esteem inhibits self-mastery. This is because 'mistakes', lessons and criticism (which are all part of the learning process) are seen as threats rather than opportunities to learn and improve.

- A focus on self-esteem impedes meaningful relationships because of the need to feel at least comparable to, if not superior to, others. This limits authentic and supportive behaviour towards others.

- Striving for self-esteem can lead to physical health problems through anxiety and stress, and to unhealthy coping behaviour to deal with low assessments of self-worth. This increases the risk of emotional eating or substance abuse.

- When we spend our precious time and energy trying to enhance the opinions others have of us, we lose the opportunity to improve ourselves in more meaningful ways. Because of the preoccupation with the expectations and standards of others, we have lost the chance to use our time and energy to fulfil our own potential.

So, here is the insight: you will feel good about yourself when you take values-driven action and achieve in an area that is important to you. Feeling good about yourself is a result of having the courage to take action, reflect, learn and grow from an experience. Feeling good about yourself comes from self-mastery and evolves as you learn and grow. That is why this book does not stop with just telling you that you are already perfect. In the next chapters, through all of the steps you will take, you will discover this for yourself through courage and action.

Remember the Seed

Let me reinforce the caution of self-esteem with a short exercise. Get yourself a piece of paper, and on one side, write down five of the helpful descriptions that you identified for yourself from Appendix 1. On the opposite side, write down five of the problematic ones. Now, go and stand in front of a mirror.

Hold the piece of paper up in front of your eyes, with the helpful descriptions facing you. Read them through and take a few minutes to soak them in. How do you feel? Is there any action you want to take? But most importantly, what has happened to your connection with the person in the mirror?

Now, do the same, but looking at the list of problematic descriptions. Again, take a few minutes to read them and become aware of the feelings that are arising for you. How do you feel now? Is there any action arising within you? But most importantly, again, what has happened to your awareness of the person in the mirror?

Now hold the piece of paper down and look at yourself in the mirror. Move the paper around in all different ways, without looking at it—noting that sometimes the list of helpful descriptions is facing upwards, and sometimes the list of problematic descriptions is shown. But do not focus on these, just concentrate on the person you see in the mirror. What is the sense of connection you have with yourself now?

The point here is, when you focus on either the positive (helpful) or negative (problematic) aspects of yourself, you lose touch with your wholeness as a person. Just like the turning of the paper, your own judgements and others' judgements of you will come and go. They will shift and change, but they are not you. Remember, they are only words describing a point in time. Recognise they are there, but focus on what matters most—the appreciation of and connection with the seed within. Understand that those words are transient and remember that the beautiful seed and its glorious potential are always within you.

The Alternative: Self-Acceptance

Self-esteem is a short-term solution to the basic human need to feel good about ourselves. However, it is outward-focused. It breeds thoughts, feelings and actions that can be self-sabotaging and destructive, which keep us at the lower Levels of Consciousness. There is a much more empowering and enduring approach to feeling good about ourselves, and this is self-acceptance. As we have heard from Dr David Hawkins in Chapter Three, acceptance is: 'The recognition of your role in the world, the ability to see the big picture of your life and the start of setting and achieving goals and living consciously and proactively to deliver on your fantastic potential.'

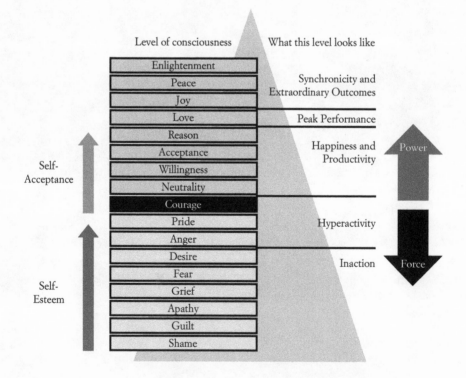

Figure 24 – The Progression of Self-Esteem to Self-Acceptance

Seeing the big picture means being able to accept all facets and attributes, being those that are positive, as well as those that you may believe are negative. To embody true self-acceptance means to be able to look at yourself in the mirror and embrace everything you see with no judgement. Self-acceptance is the recognition that you are a human being. It understands that there are some times where you will shine and other times you might feel dim. Regardless, self-acceptance calls you to continue believing in yourself and accepting yourself unconditionally. Self-acceptance acknowledges that you have areas to develop and rediscover of yourself, but it does not let that define you.

This is no easy task. We are taught that if we don't like something about ourselves, we can just change it! It is incredibly difficult to accept and be at peace with those things that we are desperate to change about ourselves. Yet, it is only by accepting ourselves where we are right now that we can begin the process of becoming who we truly are.

You have already started the journey of self-acceptance by picking up this book. You have continued along the road to self-acceptance by looking honestly at how you think and feel about yourself. You should give yourself a compliment for taking these important steps. Because, as we know, fully embracing your beauty and moving to a complete place of acceptance takes courage.

How to Get Courage

'Courage is not the absence of fear, but rather the assessment that something else is more important.'
~ Franklin D. Roosevelt

There are so many different definitions of courage, but at its most basic, it is the act of doing something that scares you. It is making a conscious decision that you will take action, despite there being a risk of the unknown. As you can see, courage identifies and concedes to a goal that is much more important than superficial praise. However, it is likely that right at this moment, you are feeling far less than courageous. I suspect you may be doubtful, or at best not feeling very confident with your ability to bloom. My response to this is—fantastic! This is exactly where you should be right now. Why? Because it shows that you are starting something new. You are moving into uncharted territory, crossing needed fields and exploring parts of yourself you have never yet discovered. Being uncomfortable right now is precisely where you need to be.

But how do you work through this discomfort and move forward? How do you get the courage you need to keep moving? While courage may be a trait that some have naturally more than others, it can be fostered. There are two basic steps to getting more courageous, and these are:

1. Take action—staying in your comfort zone does not lead to growth. If you don't do things that make you uncomfortable, you will never know what you are capable of.

2. Practise self-acceptance—recognise that you are on an unknown path. No-one has ever done what you are doing—that is, bringing your unique potential to life. So, there will be trips and falls along the way. There will be so many opportunities for learning and growth. Through them all, to gain more courage, you need to embrace every step without judgement but rather with awareness.

Without taking action, you will likely get stuck in what is known as the 'Confidence Gap'[12]—the fearful abyss between where you are now and where you want to be. When you are stuck in the Confidence Gap, you have given up on your goals and dreams. You have decided that living up to your full potential is too hard and that you don't have the confidence to build new skills. You have decided that you don't dare to move beyond the expectations of others.

What a person stuck in the Confidence Gap does not understand, though, is that courage is gained through action. In fact, the actions of confidence come first, and then the beliefs and feelings around confidence will follow. You can't just sit in the gap, praying for courage. You have to take action, reflect and learn with an open mind and an open heart.

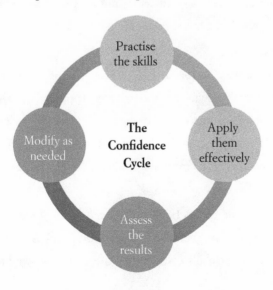

Figure 25 – The Confidence Cycle

Dr Russ Harris explains that there are five main reasons why you may find yourself stuck in the Confidence Gap, praying for courage to get out. These are[13]:

1. Lack of skills—you don't know how to do the thing that will get you across the other side, so this stops you doing anything.

2. Lack of experience—even if you do know how to do something, without practise and experience, you can feel very unprepared to take action.

3. Preoccupation with fear—fear, like every emotion, is an important messenger indicating what we value. But it is just a feeling, and this does not mean you have to buy into it and let it stop you from doing what is important.

4. Harsh self-judgment—forgetting the concept of self-acceptance and inviting in your cruel self-critic!

5. Excessive expectations—expecting miracles after taking no action is not only unrealistic, but only sets yourself up for more self-criticism.

The first two of these factors are fixed through action. If you don't know how to do something—then take action to learn. If you don't feel like you have enough experience, then take action to practise. There is a very simple process to learning, and this applies whether you are learning to walk, show up in your swimwear with no cover top required or to bloom into your beauty. Here it is:

If you reach the end of this book and tell me that you are not getting the results you had hoped for, then the first question I will ask you is how you have been practising the skills and tailoring them to your own life. As I have said before, the process of blooming is not a theoretical one. It takes courage, commitment and action. You may have denied yourself for so very long that it will take time and practise to find your true self again.

There are so many myths and stories we tell ourselves about fear. For example, that it is a sign of weakness, or that when you are confident you don't have any doubt. None of these are true! Here is the simple truth: when you step out of your comfort zone, take a risk or face a challenge, you will feel fear. It is not a weakness. It's the natural state for human beings. We have a brain that wants to keep us safe, to protect us, which naturally will hold us back from the unknown.

So, fear is an entirely normal emotion when you are going beyond what you already know. Fear is not the problem, what is actually holding you back is the belief you have towards it. Do you try to push fear away? Do you try to suppress the fear? Do you say harsh and harmful judgments to yourself for feeling fear? I know it sounds contrary to everything you have ever been told. But the only way to cross the Confidence Gap is to embrace and lean in to fear as a sign of moving forward to change and achieve. Everything you want in your life is on the other side of that fear.

It is the same for the harsh self-judgements and unrealistic expectations that we set on ourselves. These limiting beliefs and stories are created by our mind to keep us safe. So you can happily know that they are a sign that your mind is doing its job! But is the safe little spot you are in now really where you want to be?

In Chapter 16, we will go through some techniques you can use to defuse negative thoughts as they arise. But for now, commit yourself to courage, commit yourself to action and commit yourself to self-acceptance. Because I want to show you the next level of possibility for you, and that is living in the light of self-compassion.

But first, here are some questions to help you move forward into self-acceptance. I believe self-acceptance is embodied in living consciously and actively to fulfill your tremendous potential. What are some of the conscious and proactive things that you will be doing when you are operating from acceptance? What would you be doing in the areas of:

- Health—physical and mental;

- Finance—spending, saving and investing;

- Career and education;

- Family and friendships; and

- Spirituality and contribution.

How do you currently deal with criticism of others both:

- Immediately with the other person?

- Afterwards when you are by yourself?

Think of an area of life where you feel stuck between where you are now, and where you want to be. What are the things that are holding you back?

- Skills—is there anything you need to learn?

- Experience—is there anything you need more time practising?

- Fear—do you have concerns about what success might mean and the opinions of other people?

- Self-judgement— do you have concerns about how you see yourself?

- Expectations—do you have any unrealistic and unfair expectations about what you can achieve?

WHAT NEXT?

While there is much focus on self-esteem, it provides an unbalanced view of yourself. Self-esteem concentrates on only the positive elements of our being, which is unrealistic, and also unfair. Aiming for self-esteem places so much pressure on us to get everything right and to fit into other people's expectations. A much kinder, healthier and more mature approach is self-acceptance. Acceptance works with reality—who you are just as you are. It recognises that we are all a mix of helpful and unwanted traits, and there may be things that we need to improve on to grow and bloom. But this does not mean we respect ourselves any less.

Far from accepting being a 'cop-out', it takes great courage. It is a bold and brave move to look at ourselves honestly and to take action on those things that are hindering our growth and preventing us from being the best we can be. Taking action does not require you to feel confident first. The small actions you take day by day will create momentum and energy, and help you to build confidence. You just need to begin. Because the next leap is waiting for you—it is the leap from self-acceptance to self-compassion. This leap moves you to a place where you can love yourself as you would a friend, and where you become your own best friend. Self-compassion is the next level of maturity, where you use your innate power and wisdom to work towards removing your own suffering and ensuring your own happiness.

COMMITMENT STATEMENT

I commit to acknowledging, respecting and caring for myself as a whole person, without criticism and without judgement.

I commit to live consciously, proactively and to fulfil my great potential.

CHAPTER TWELVE

From Acceptance to Compassion

'If you want others to be happy, practise compassion.
If you want to be happy, practise compassion.'
~ Dalai Lama

What is Self-Compassion?

Self-acceptance is the first step to refeeding your own beautiful blooming and operating from a place of happiness and productivity. Self-acceptance recognises and respects our whole self without judgement. Then, self-compassion is the step that will help you bloom, thrive from a place of love and peace, and achieve extraordinary outcomes. What do I mean by self-compassion? Let's begin with the definition of what compassion is:

'Compassion is the sense of care and concern we have when we notice someone else's suffering, and the motivation to relieve that suffering[14].'

When you see a girl being bullied because of her appearance, or a friend struggling with confidence because of how she feels about how she looks, and you want to reach out and ease their pain, then this is compassion. Compassion recognises that it is the natural human condition to experience pain and suffering, and responds with kindness, understanding and patience. Compassion responds with love, wanting the best for the person that is hurting, not out of fear, pride or seeking to protect your status or sense of self-worth. Let's apply this to the Levels of Consciousness as you will see next.

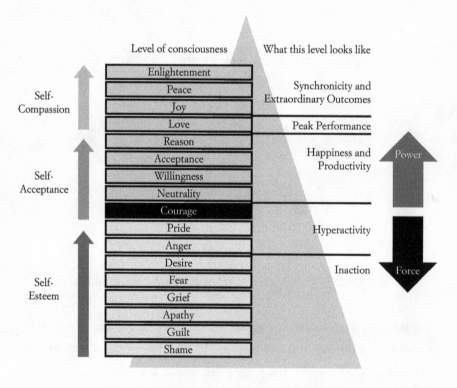

Figure 26 – The Progression of Acceptance to Compassion

What Does Self-Compassion Look Like?

Having compassion for yourself does not look any different to showing compassion for someone else. Only the recipient of the compassion changes and it is you. Let's break down the flow of feelings and actions we would see:

1. First is the awareness of suffering. To have compassion for others, you must first be able to notice that they are suffering. To have compassion for yourself, you also have to notice when you are having a difficult time. You notice this when you are experiencing a thought that drains you, or when you are worrying about something you have to do or don't like about yourself. You may be tempted to react by telling yourself to 'toughen up' or 'get over it'. But self-compassion calls you to acknowledge the discomfort or pain you are experiencing.

2. Second, come the feelings of compassion. This involves allowing the emotions of care and kindness to arise and acknowledging the desire you may have to help the person suffering in some way. Feeling compassion can hurt because you are opening your heart to the pain and allowing yourself to feel. Compassion doesn't offer any judgement, only understanding and the motivation to act—to be of assistance to relieve the pain.

This second step takes an incredible amount of courage because it is allowing yourself to truly and fully feel the pain you are experiencing. It does not brush aside difficult emotions, but respects them, holds them and cares for them as part of your reality in that moment.

Self-compassion does not judge your emotions as a sign of being 'too sensitive' or 'weak'. Self-compassion does not tell you to stop crying or that you are overreacting. Self-compassion sits with the 'uncomfortable' feelings. It looks into them and acknowledges how difficult things are for you at that moment. Then it goes further to identify how you can comfort and care for yourself in that moment. Do you need silence, space and time? Do you need the beauty of nature? Do you need the voice of a supportive friend? Or do you just need to sleep? Self-compassion finds a way to help you relieve your suffering in positive and healthy ways—in ways that will care for your future health and wellbeing.

3. Finally, compassion recognises that pain, suffering, failure and imperfection are universal—that they are part of the shared experience of being human. It does not seek to place you in any superior or inferior position, or any place of being luckier or unluckier than anyone else. It recognises that all humans have difficult times.

This last step, the acknowledgement of universal suffering, is one that is often missed but is vital to complete the full cycle of self-compassion. If you miss the step of acknowledging your suffering and pain as part of the bigger human condition, then you run the risk of over-identifying with your problems and falling into the traps of self-consciousness, self-esteem and narcissism. This is when you begin to focus on your problems, your difficulties, and lose sight of your role in the bigger picture—your connection with others—and strive only for the relief of your suffering. By honouring and accepting your humanity, and understanding your feelings are shared throughout the world, then your blooming becomes part of a much broader and more meaningful outcome. Your blooming then becomes about sharing your gifts with the world, rather than just making yourself feel good.

In this way, self-compassion holds a sense of intrinsic self-worth that is stable and not beaten around by the perceptions of others or the judgements we place on ourselves. It does not increase with successes or decrease with less-than thoughts. It remains a constant companion to help you be the best you can be.

What Self-Compassion is Not

Self-compassion can be confused with many other concepts. So, it is best to make exact explicits of what it is not in order to ensure there is no misunderstanding and misguided action.

Self-compassion is not self-esteem. Self-compassion does not require that we see ourselves positively, or that others see ourselves positively either. In fact, self-compassion kicks in when self-esteem has gone, and we are left feeling less than. Self-compassion does not just exist when we meet our own or others' expectations, or when we 'win'. Self-compassion exists in our highest and our lowest moments and is there to see us through both. It exists when we have no self-esteem or positive self-image to draw on. It exists independently of whatever our current level of self-esteem may be.

Self-compassion is not judgement. Self-compassion does not judge if we are shining or wilting. And even more than that, self-compassion sees the perfect seed within us and cares about that. It reaches out not in judgement or criticism. Instead, it embraces us with kindness, connectedness and balance, no matter what the situation is. It reaches out with care and warmth, not self-flagellation and punishment. Self-compassion allows us to feel compassion towards ourselves. Not because someone else decided we deserve it, but because as human beings, we are worthy of respect and understanding.

Self-compassion is not pity. There is a very small but very important distinction between self-compassion and self-pity. Self-pity sees suffering but acts out of anger, fear or guilt. Self-compassion sees the suffering but acts out of love and the genuine concern to relieve hurt and enable reaching your full potential. For example, one person at the dinner table may watch a girl who is living with anorexia struggling to eat their meal, and feel anger that the hard work they put into the meal is being disrespected. They may ask difficult questions about her enjoyment of the meal or her level of hunger. However, another person may ask the girl to help her clear the plates, out of the concern to take her away from an awkward situation and to make her feel better. Do you see how the actions of the first person were motivated by anger? But the act of inviting the girl to help clear the plates was driven by genuine care about how the girl was feeling. That is the difference between compassion and pity. And self-compassion is the greatest gift you can give to yourself.

Self-compassion is not indulgence. There is active resistance by some to self-compassion because they feel that they would be letting themselves 'off the hook' or permitting themselves to partake in indulgent activities. For example, say you have had a rough day at work. You come home feeling deflated and beaten. Self-indulgence would say something like, 'You have had a rough day; have a couple of glasses of wine and a tub of chocolate ice cream. You deserve it!' Whereas self-compassion cares for you well past that moment of despair. It looks to the future and knows that if you drink that wine and eat that ice cream, you may feel even worse and not do other activities that will help you deal with the stress in a more self-sustaining way. So, self-compassion may say something like, 'You have had a very rough day. I can see how tired you are and how you just want to drown your sorrows in wine and ice cream. But I suspect after such a tough day you are not thinking so clearly at the moment. How about you have a bath, and I will sit with you and work through this discomfort and if wine and ice cream do make you truly feel good—let's do it all!' In this way, self-compassion does not try to just numb or distract you from the feelings of pain and hurt and provide short-term pleasure. It helps you hold them with care, and it cares about your long-term health and wellbeing and supports your seed's nourishment.

Why is Self-Compassion a Skill?

It is a very curious phenomenon that we can muster deep levels of compassion for people around us, yet we find it so very difficult to respond the same way to ourselves. We seem to believe that we require more harsh and negative treatment than that we give others. From what we have learned, it may be explained by our operating from fear, guilt, shame or pride, motivating our actions, rather than courage, love and self-acceptance.

Everyone will have their backstory to explain this dichotomy of compassion. Still, the result is clear: if we want to be able to turn the light of compassion on to ourselves, then we need to apply the Confidence Cycle to this as well. We need to take action, reflect and modify our actions to get better at self-compassion. If self-compassion does not come naturally to you now, then just like any new skill, it will take practise. When you learn an instrument, you find a teacher and practise every day. It is no different when you are learning self-compassion. Self-compassion, when it is embedded in your daily life, is the sun that will draw you upwards to the blooming of your full potential.

How Would You Treat a Friend?

It is so interesting! You would think that loving yourself would be the easiest activity. After all, you live with yourself every day and, in the end, we are all we have. But, turning inwards and showing compassion to ourselves is one of the hardest things for us to do. But, just like any skill we want to learn, all it takes is practise. So, let's begin with one small exercise. This exercise calls on you to become aware of the different approach you take towards the suffering of others and your own pain. To gain this awareness, work through the following questions:

1. Bring to mind a time when a friend was struggling and feeling bad about themselves. What did you do? What did you say? But more importantly, how did you do and say these things? What tone did you use? What was your body language like? How did you feel at that moment?

2. Next, bring to mind a time when you were feeling bad about yourself and were struggling. What did you do? What did you say? But more importantly, how did you do and say these things? What tone did you use? What was your body language like? How did you feel at that moment?

3. Did you notice any difference between how you responded to the struggles of a friend compared to the way you responded to your own struggles? If there were differences, can you identify what factors, beliefs or feelings came into play that led you to treat yourself differently?

4. Now, replay the situation in step two, where you were struggling. But instead of responding the way you did, replace this with the words and actions you shared with your friend in step one. If you held your friend, then hug yourself too. If you held their hand, then hold yours. Say the same words of care you shared with your friend with yourself. How did this feel? Did it come easily, or did you feel some barriers?

This activity is just the very beginning of becoming aware of the different levels of compassion we have for ourselves and others. We will expand on it later, but for now, I will leave you with this thought: What might happen if you treat yourself like a good friend?

When Self-Compassion Hurts

I will not try and delude you by saying that self-compassion is necessarily a pleasant experience. Honestly acknowledging, feeling and caring for your discomfort can really get uncomfortable. That is why it takes so much courage and practise. It is easier to distract yourself from your feelings of distress and dismiss your pain. The way people become stuck in the roller-coaster of self-esteem is understandable. It takes an awful lot of guts to move beyond the views of others, to go deep and become the ultimate carer for yourself. In some way, caring for others is easier because their pain is somewhat removed from us. When we sit with our own, there is no barrier and we cannot leave it and go home. It is with us until we can acknowledge it, love it and let it go.

This process can take a tremendously long time. I have hurts that I feel like I have been caring for my whole life. Some days, dealing with these emotions starts bringing me down. Living with this pain, while necessary, can get heavy and, if left unchecked, can bring you down too. So how do you regain more balance if self-compassion becomes too weighty? What is the antidote to the pain? The antidotes are appreciation and joy.

Appreciation is the process of recognising and appreciating all of the gifts and blessings you have around you. To prevent you from getting stuck in your suffering, turn your mind to all the wonderful qualities you have and all the people and things you have around you that help you every day. Yes, there is suffering and pain, but there are also many gifts you have to help you deal with these challenges. You have your own wonderful virtues. You have food, shelter, inspirational teachers and the sun in the sky to brighten your day. You have a hot cup of tea or chocolate, and you have a hug from a friend or with a pet. Lift yourself out of suffering and take some time to see the miracles that are within you and around you.

Just as you can appreciate the good things in your life, you can also celebrate the virtues and achievements of others. Reading an inspirational biography reminds you of the virtues of people you admire. Watching a movie about overcoming adversity can help you celebrate the tenacity of others. Talking with friends can remind you how much you appreciate their wisdom. Revelling in the qualities of others and in their pleasure will help you balance the weight of compassion. This is the practice of joy. Each one of these things is a cause for celebration, as it reminds you of the good things that are in the world and in other people. It will provide the cheerleading you need along the way to keep you moving towards flourishing.

Here are some reflection questions to help you live in the light of self-compassion. Think about a person that you believe shows high levels of compassion, not only to others but also to themselves. Take a moment to describe:

- The person's physical appearance—what they look like, their facial expressions, how they sit and how they move.

- The person's voice—the words they use and the tone and style of their language.

- What they do—what is it about this person that tells you they have self-compassion?

- How do you feel—when you are around this person what emotions and feelings come up for you?

What do you think would happen if you treated yourself with the same care and compassion that this person treats themselves and others?

Another valuable exercise is to list three things that you are appreciative for about this day, and about yourself. This may be difficult at first, but I would highly recommend that you take some time to do this at the end of each day. You might also like to list three things that bring you joy. For each one, think about how you may be able to get more of these things into your every day.

WHAT NEXT?

Self-compassion is the practice that will help you to live consciously, peacefully and freely in your skin. It enables you to love yourself wholly and completely. Loving yourself is more than just a nice feeling; loving yourself is about taking action. When you love yourself, you work actively to relieve your own suffering and create space, support and behaviours that bring joy and appreciation for who you are.

There are things you can do every day to practise self-compassion and to express love and care for yourself. One of these is to set up an environment that will support you to feel good, build great habits and, when you need to, provide a place for peaceful retreat. The space you create for yourself will shape you. It will influence your mood, motivation and even physical health. People have varying levels of control over the spaces in which they live and work. However, there is always something you can do, no matter how minor, to enact self-compassion, right where you are. Creating a positive physical space is the compassionate action we will take in the next chapter.

COMMITMENT STATEMENT

I commit to caring for myself as I would my best friend. I commit to taking action to relieve my suffering and embedding behaviours that support my flourishing.

CHAPTER THIRTEEN

Your Growth Environment: Physical Space

'Be careful of the environment you choose,
for it will shape you.'
~ W. Clement Stone

How Your Physical Environment Affects You

If you have experienced the joy of gardening before, you will know that the location plays a significant role in a plant's ability to thrive. If a seed is planted in soil with the wrong level of acidity or a temperature that is either too warm or too cold, it will not germinate. It will stay dormant until it is in a type of soil that it knows will support its future growth. Once the plant has sprouted, it needs sunlight each day and space for its roots to grow and leaves to breathe. Seeds planted in a soil that is not right for its type will not germinate. Plants will not thrive and flowers will not bloom unless they are in an environment that suits their nature.

It is the same for you. Your environment plays a critical supporting role to your blooming. An environment that matches your nature, your true beliefs and your goals will lift you and move you forward. An environment that is misaligned to the needs of the unique and beautiful you will keep you dormant or trapped in patterns of unhealthy behaviour.

Like the seed, though, you may not be completely aware of the impact the environment has on you. We all go about our days largely on autopilot. But your surroundings—at home and at work, as well as where you shop, exercise and study—directly affect your levels of stress, mood, motivation and relationships.

Let me provide an example by way of a study that was done in a hospital cafeteria to improve healthy eating[15]. A two-stage experiment was conducted. The first involved labelling all of the food in the cafeteria with a green, red or yellow sticker. Green stickers indicated a healthy food choice, yellow a neutral item and red stickers showed unhealthy food choices. Signs were put up around the cafeteria, explaining the colour coding. This signage highlighted that green meant 'consume often', yellow meant 'consume less often', and red meant 'there is a better choice in green or yellow'. There was no negative messaging telling people not to eat the red items. Instead, they were supported with a positive message that there were better choices available to them. In this first stage, everyone was aware of how the environment was helping them make food choices. It was probably no surprise that the sale of healthy items increased during this time, and the sale of unhealthy foods decreased.

But the second stage was even more interesting. Without telling people, foods were moved around the cafeteria to improve the visibility and convenience of the green items. This included replacing soda in the fridges with water, placing sandwiches and snacks at eye level and moving red items out of the line of direct vision. So, while the first stage was completely conscious, these choices being made in the second stage were much more unconscious. In this second stage, the environment was shaping their decisions. The results? Again, the purchase of green items increased and the sale of foods with red stickers decreased significantly. The biggest result was seen in the consumption of water and soft drinks. Just look at the graph below to see the marked improvement in water consumption and the significant reduction in soft drink consumption from this experiment.

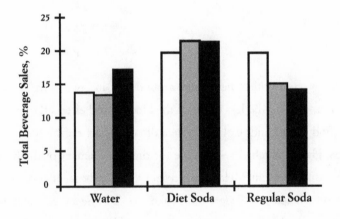

Figure 27 – Changes to Beverage Consumption with Label and Architecture Intervention

This study clearly shows two things:

1. We can set up our environment to help us make supportive choices every day that will help us care for our bodies, minds and spirits.

2. We need to be aware of how others are using these techniques to sway us towards choices that don't support our wellbeing or goals.

Elements of Your Physical Environment

However, it is not just what you see around you that has an impact. Your environment is full of sensory cues that affect your mood and motivation. What you hear, touch and smell also can significantly influence your view of the world and the positivity you bring to daily challenges. Here are some of the key elements of your physical environment that are worth paying some attention to.

Colour

While you may notice the colours around you and note whether you like them or not, you may be less aware of the biochemical effects they are having on your body and mind. Colours have a direct impact on the functioning of the pineal gland, which is responsible for the management of the hormones melatonin and serotonin. Melatonin is responsible for the feelings of sleepiness, and serotonin helps us feel alert and awake. You may be aware that melatonin imbalances are related to sleep disturbances and serotonin imbalances with mood disorders. This relationship stemmed from our early existence in the natural environment when our bodies were activated by the yellow light of day and subdued dark-blue light of the evening.

The message here is that the colours around us do affect our body, mind and spirit. They can be used consciously to help us find the energy and motivation we need or to create a place of peace where we can come back to rest and restore. Warm colours are generally helpful when there is a symptom of weakness, such as fatigue. Cool colours are beneficial where there is a symptom of excess, such as stress.

Here is an overview of the power of colours prepared by Vanderbilt University[16]:

Colour	Psychological and Emotional Effects	Physical Effects Effects
Red	Energy, empowerment and stimulation	Circulation and stimulation of red blood cell production
Orange	Pleasure and enthusiasm	Antibacterial agent and to ease digestive discomforts
Yellow	Wisdom and clarity	Decongestant, antibacterial agent and support for the digestive and lymphatic systems
Green	Balance and calmness	Support for ulcers, as an antiseptic and as an antibacterial agent
Blue	Communication and knowledge	Eliminate toxins, and to treat liver disorders and jaundice
Indigo	Sedative qualities, calmness and intuition	Control bleeding and abscesses
Violet	Enlightenment, revelation and spiritual awakening	Soothe organs, relax muscles and calm the nervous system

Of course, holistic health practitioners have known about the power of colours well before they were proven by science. The theory and treatment of chakras (energy centres in the body) revolves around the concept that there are areas of the body which resonate on the same energy vibration as specific colours. When a problem is identified in a specific area of the body, then the associated colour for this muscle or organ can be used to heal and rebalance the chakra.

Light

We have seen that the colours that surround you can help encourage feelings of strength, empowerment or tranquillity, all of which are needed along this great journey of blooming. Sunlight is one of nature's gifts and has been shown to have a direct impact on your health. However, when you are considering improving your health and vitality, it is important to note that not all sunlight is equal. It has been found that morning light reduces stress and depression and increases alertness[17]. So room designs and lifestyle routines that engage the morning sun will inevitably contribute to improved mood and motivation.

Noise

The amount and type of noise you experience in your environment can impact your physical health or frame of mind and, therefore, your ability to grow and bloom. Both acute and chronic noise events trigger a physiological stress response in your body. Noise can trigger the release of stress hormones such as adrenaline and cortisol. Noise negatively impacts so many systems in the body, including the immune system and endocrine system. It has this effect due to its disturbance of:

- Communication—noise makes it harder to hear what someone else is saying, creating a concern of missing important information.
- Attention—noise negatively affects the mental processes of concentration.
- Sleep—either by disrupting the ability to get to sleep or causing awakening during the sleep cycle.
- Emotion—some sounds trigger stressful emotions such as fear and anger. These feelings are exacerbated if the noise has interrupted the other functions, such as communication, concentration or sleep.

Ultimately, unwanted noise in our environments creates an annoyance that can disrupt our days and our level of positivity. Being annoyed at the noise around you creates feelings at the very least of displeasure and discomfort and at the worst of resentment and rage. This mental and emotional annoyance also has negative impacts on our physical wellbeing, which can create a downward cycle of unhelpful thoughts and behaviours. Leaving the space, soundproofing or using noise-reducing earphones are all strategies that can help remove unwanted noises.

In contrast, also think about how some sounds can help to bring a different energy to your space. Uplifting music can help ignite and inspire. Sounds of waterfalls and wind can help create a sense of movement. Then there is the joy of silence. Sounds can work with you or against you. It is just a matter of becoming aware and taking conscious action to create an environment that is best for you.

Your Digital Environment

No longer do we only spend time in physical places. So much of our time now is also spent in the digital world. We work and socialise through many different social media and electronic channels. While this technology creates an incredible amount of opportunity to engage and connect, there is one important thing to consider when you are in the digital environment: that it is very difficult to tap into the emotions of others. When we are interacting in the same physical space with others and face-to-face, we can read emotions and respond accordingly. But this is very difficult to do digitally, and this creates greater uncertainty and stress.

Also, when you are operating online, you naturally become more concerned with how you are being perceived. It is the task network of the brain that manages your interactions on social media, and this network is largely concerned with evaluation and judgement of our performance. In this way, the digital world inherently creates a situation of social comparison. Spending a vast amount of time in the social comparison or evaluative mode of functioning creates a significant amount of stress and worry. In short, social media might give you a short-term hit of excitement. But staying in this unnatural world for too long is likely to keep you in the lower levels of consciousness and keep you comparing yourself with others. With social media, it can be easy to fall into the trap of trying to fit in, but you were definitely made to stand out in this world.

Clutter

In recent times a light has been cast on the negative impact that physical clutter has not only on your productivity, but also your physical and mental state. Clutter creates an incredible distraction. Just like noise, this distraction makes it difficult to process information, to concentrate and to learn, and ultimately leads to frustration and exhaustion. Even more worrying, clutter reduces the level of control that you feel you have over your life. In turn, this impacts on your level of resilience and can result in emotional distress. It does appear that the adage holds true that 'cleanliness is next to godliness'.

Clutter, of course, is not only found in our physical spaces but in our digital environment as well. How many unread emails do you have? When was the last time you cleaned up your desktop or online files? For many of us, clutter and chaos is occurring on several devices, such as a computer, phone and tablet.

If nothing is done about clutter, then it continues to distract and depress and before you know it, you can be on a downward spiral to a lack of confidence and despair. It may be easier right now to think that you are too busy to deal with it, or that you don't know where to start. However, avoiding it only increases the mess physically, mentally and emotionally.

So, if you want to show care and compassion for yourself, then clean up your clutter! Declutter and get organised. Show yourself how much you love yourself by giving yourself a clutter-free space to live in, work in and become the best you.

The Key Issue: Lack of Control

Across all of these environmental elements, there is one fundamental difference between an uncomfortable and comfortable space: the level of control you have over it. Feeling like you don't have any decision over the colours, noises, views or mess around you is a key trigger for confidence issues. But this does not mean there is nothing you can do to create an environment that will help you feel safe, comfortable and supported to shine.

Create Your Sanctuary

The aim of creating a *Body Beautiful* space is to reduce stress. For it is the stress that will prevent you from thinking well, feeling well and making the best choices for your precious time and energy. The stress caused by your environment can keep you stuck and unable to sprout.

While it may be fun to imagine a full house redesign, the recommendation is to start small. As shown in the Confidence Cycle, the most important thing is to take some action, reflect and learn. So, choose one room or a corner that you can make into your little sanctuary. It could be a spare room or a corner of your bedroom. If you can, find a space that has good natural light and, if possible, a view of the natural world. These will help to uplift and inspire you.

Then think about the activities you find empowering and affirming. It could be yoga, reading, painting or doing jigsaw puzzles. Adapt your space to include these activities—for example, by putting your yoga mat and props in this space, putting in a comfy chair and easel or setting up a jigsaw table. What sounds do you like to hear? A water fountain may be nice to help you unwind and reflect on your day. What smells give you the support you are looking for? Maybe lemongrass to invigorate or lavender to calm. What colours do you like to have around you? Maybe you might have a few different coloured shawls available, and choose one to wrap yourself in that provides the energy you need on the day. Do you need bright light to help you see for reading or craft, or dull light for meditation?

This sanctuary is more than just a fun exercise. It is about confirming to you that you do have control over both your external environment and inner world. You can take actions that help you manage the stresses and the strains around you, and you can change your world both outside and in. You can care for yourself and create the space you need to grow and bloom. You can show yourself love and compassion. This sanctuary is a symbol of your awareness of how you feel, acceptance of where you are and concern to ease your own suffering. It is a symbol of how you are learning and practising the skills of caring for yourself and your unique and amazing potential. If you would like to, you can open your sanctuary with a little ceremony where you set a conscious intention for the space.

Okay, I understand that for some, the ability to create your own space in the house is a pipedream. Your circumstances just don't provide the privacy or level of control you need to allocate and keep a special place of your own. This situation is difficult for so many reasons. The lack of agency over your physical environment exacerbates any battles you are having with your unique spirit and your body. Feeling like you don't have any control over your environment can cause great discomfort and inhibit your identity. In turn, this can impact on your confidence to make changes for your wellbeing.

But I will repeat my view: if you are committed to your health and growth, and if you are dedicated to being at peace with your body and your spirit, there is always something you can do. To prove this point, let me give you an example from a friend whose space is continually raided by adventurous and creative kids. She has given up the battles with trying to have a set space that is her private sanctuary. Instead, she has a mobile one. This is her yoga mat. She moves her yoga mat around to capture the sun and silence. It may end up on the deck with the sunrise. It may come out in the study while the children have their afternoon naps. It may be unrolled beside her bed before sleep.

You see, yoga is the way she connects with her body. She has learned that feeling strong and flexible in her body also gives her an inner sense of courage and adaptability. On her mat, she chooses strength poses to build confidence in her body or restorative poses to provide time for reconnection. After this, if she has time, she lays on her mat and reads or listens to an empowering podcast. It does not matter where the mat is located. It is the act of being on it that counts. Time on this mat is the way she honours her body as the home for her unique seed.

The Importance of Nature

If there were only one thing you could do to help you bloom, then it would be spending time in nature. We are fundamentally organic beings, formed from the same substances as the natural world. So it is not surprising that being in natural landscapes and participating in wilderness experiences have a significant positive effect on our health and wellbeing.

As outlined in the book *Healing Gardens*[18], researchers found that more than two-thirds of people found that natural settings offer an effective retreat when stressed. In another study published in *Mind*, 94 per cent of respondents reported that spending time outdoors helped their moods shift to calmness and a sense of balance[19]. Being in nature has a magical way of reversing the effects of stress, including lowering blood pressure, reducing heart rate and easing muscle tension. These physical changes directly improve our sense of wellbeing. They reduce problematic emotions, such as anger and fear. Our connection with and interest for natural forms also distracts us from pain and boosts our levels of curiosity and creativity.

More than just the reduction of stress, being in nature plays a vital role in creating a sense of meaning. It enables you to feel a part of something bigger than yourself, which some people associate with spirituality. Whatever label you put on it, an MRI study has shown that viewing nature activates the parts of the brain that are related to empathy and love—that is, the higher levels of consciousness[20]. It makes us feel a connection with the environment, with others and also with ourselves. Interestingly, the same MRI study showed that when the participants viewed scenes of city life, the parts of the brain that help manage fear and anxiety were activated. This proved that being in nature reduces stress and creates a feeling of altruism.

The good news is that you can have the benefits of nature in your own home. Research found that just having one plant in a room associates with having the natural world near you, which activates feelings of calm, groundedness and belonging[21].

Nature Can Enhance Body Image

Have you ever been on an outdoor or wilderness adventure? Have you ever been rock climbing, mountaineering or tried forest obstacle courses? These kinds of activities have been shown to directly counteract negative body image because, for that exercise, the emphasis is placed on the body's capabilities, not appearance[22]. Using the strength and agility of the body gives a greater respect for the awesome gift that our body is, and places the priority on what the body can do, not what it looks like. In a way, using our bodies in the outdoors brings us back to what is truly important about our bodies.

What research also shows, is that the positive effects of outdoor adventures don't end when you leave the forest. Incredibly, girls who participated in outdoor adventure programs still felt a positive influence on their body image three years later. This is because outdoor adventures provide the space and time for participants to challenge the beauty norms they are faced with in their everyday lives. Getting covered in dirt and testing the capabilities of your body lessens the importance of appearance and gets you back in touch with your strength and power. Having others around you doing this too creates an inspiration to focus on healthy lifestyles and what the body can do for you in your journey to bloom.

Here are some quotes from girls participating in a study on the effects of outdoor adventures on body image:

- 'When I was hiking, I couldn't care less about how I looked or what people thought.'

- 'I feel so much healthier.'

- 'I learned that my body can withstand a lot—for example, when I did hiking. I was almost positive I would not reach the top, but I did in the end.'

- 'I learned that it doesn't matter what your body image is because if you just put your mind to it, you can do it.'

There would be no better time than in this stage of The Expedition to head out on an outdoor adventure. What do you think?

Here are some questions to help you consider the role of your environment in supporting the unique and beautiful you. Make a list of the spaces you spend most of your time in. For example, this may be your home more generally, or the kitchen or your bedroom more specifically. It could also be a workplace or study environment. Perhaps you care for others in their home. For each space, think about the following:

Space		
How do I feel in this space?		
What do I notice about the colour in this space?		
What do I notice about the noise in this space?		
Is there access to bright or natural light here?		
What is the level of tidiness in this space?		

Where are the places you feel most free to be yourself?

Do you think creating a sanctuary would be of benefit for you? If so, spend some time designing this space. Firstly, what activities would you like to be doing in this sanctuary? What colours would you use for the walls? What flooring would you use? What furniture or textiles would make this space special for you? What lighting and sounds would you like to have? Design a sanctuary to give you what you need to grow into your unique beauty. Then make it happen!

Reflect on the experiment done in the hospital cafeteria. What healthy habits are you working on for yourself now? How could you design your environment to support these habits? For example, instead of putting fruit in the fridge, could you leave some on the kitchen bench? Could you put your sports clothes beside your bed at night to make it easier for you to choose to walk in the morning? Could you rearrange your room to help you wake up with the first rays of the sun?

WHAT NEXT?

The physical spaces we live, work and play in can provide such a supportive role for us. And if we are conscious of them we can take care to manage, where we can, those elements of the environment that are stunting our growth. Likewise, now we know that the natural environment is interwoven with our health and wellbeing and can help us establish a positive body image. We can choose wisely and consciously to engage with Mother Nature even more.

It is in this same spirit of consciousness and wisdom that we move forward to consider now the role of our social environment for our confidence and our wellbeing and growth. The environment that can help or hinder your growth is not just composed of physical spaces, but also the people that are in them. Even the most beautiful temples can be tainted by those who disrespect the space. Likewise, bitter winds and frost can stunt a seed, even if it is planted in the right soil. With the care of people who provide nurturing support for its potential, the seed has a great chance of making it to flower and sharing its beauty with the world. Let's see how your personal relationships may be assisting your growth journey.

COMMITMENT STATEMENT

I commit to bringing consciousness into my physical and digital spaces and using these resources to support me to bloom.

CHAPTER FOURTEEN

Your Growth Environment: Personal Relationships

'Be careful the friends you choose for you will become like them.'

~ W. Clement Stone

We have seen how influential our personal and social networks have been in shaping our current beliefs and behaviours. Growing up, you needed to fit in to make sure you were cared for and protected by your tribe. However, now you are grown up, you have much greater control over who you interact with and who you don't. You have more power to determine who you will share your time and energy with. Moreover, the relationships that may have helped you survive until this point are not necessarily those that are going to help you thrive in the future.

There is a very famous saying by Jim Rohn that states: 'You're the average of the five people you spend the most time with.' Who are the five people you spend the most time with, and how would you describe them? Are these the kind of relationships you would like for yourself? How much are the people you spend time with like the person you want to be? How much are these people living the life you have envisaged for yourself?

Before now, you may not have stopped to think about who you surround yourself with. We tend to stick to family obligations, even if these relationships become unhelpful or are unsupportive. We fall into social groups that are not often reviewed for how they fit with our future. The fact is, though, the network you spend time in has a direct influence on both your physical and mental wellbeing. So, to move forward and to bloom, it is time to investigate how your current social community is influencing your ability to achieve your best and brightest future.

Influences on Body and Mind

I remember my parents telling me on several occasions not to hang around with 'this friend' or 'that boy' because they were a 'bad influence'. At the time I thought they were just talking nonsense, but the longer I have lived, the more I realise they were very right. There is even comprehensive research that supports their assertion. Studies with women aged eighteen–thirty found that when they viewed positive body images from their Facebook network, their body image and mood improved[23]. However, when presented with idealised or appearance-neutral posts, women were more likely to experience heightened concerns about their body image and appearance[24]. So, it is not only your friends' perceptions of body image that has an influence on you, but your wider network—the friends of your friends—affect how you feel about your body as well. This broad network is directly accessible through social media, and the images you see can either help or hinder your journey.

A longitudinal study was undertaken over twenty years and found that if a close friend becomes happy, then it increases the likelihood that you will be happy by 25 per cent[25]. If a sibling is happy, then you are 14 per cent more likely to be happy yourself. Surprisingly, if your next-door neighbour is happy, then you have a whopping 34 per cent greater likelihood of being happy. Just like we have seen with perceptions of body image, happiness also has three degrees of separation. If a friend of a friend of your friend is happy, then it increases your likelihood of happiness by 6 per cent. You may think that this increase in happiness is only trivial. However, when offered a $10,000 pay rise, most people's level of happiness only increases by 2 per cent, so the influence of happy social networks is significantly greater than monetary incentives.

So, there you go. There is proof that my parents were right. They have the perfect opportunity now to say, 'I told you so.' Both positive and negative body image and happiness spread in social networks. So, just imagine what else you may be picking up from your friends and family without even being aware of it.

Why does it occur, though? Researchers believe it has to do with social norms. If your friend is constantly judging their body based on what they see on social media, then you make an evaluation, largely unconsciously, that this is acceptable behaviour. Therefore, your behaviour changes to fit the norm. In this way, your beliefs of what is acceptable are based on those that you see around you. If your friends and their contacts are positive and optimistic, you come to believe that this also should be the norm of behaviour. The result? You adjust your actions to fit the positive and optimistic standard around you.

There is a very important message here: If you want to be comfortable in your skin, if you want to bloom and celebrate your unique beauty, then it is crucial that you find a community that fosters acceptance and compassion for themselves. A network of people around you who live intentionally and share their great potential with the world will give you a good head start to achieving this yourself.

What Unhelpful Relationships Look Like

There may be people in your life right now that you feel some sense of obligation or commitment to, but they just don't feel aligned to the *Body Beautiful* journey you are on. It can be hard to identify what might be causing the discomfort. Still, ultimately it comes down to the fact that they are working from the lower levels of consciousness, which you are working to move away from. As we have seen, your community has so much influence over both your physical and mental state. If the people around you are living predominantly from shame, fear, guilt, anger, pride and desire, then it is likely that you will be too.

What are the signs that your family or friends could be living from the lower levels of consciousness? Here are some good clues:

- They are jealous. Jealousy is shown by excessive competition and diminishing your accomplishments. This behaviour indicates that this person is living with the fear of not being good enough and is motivated by self-esteem rather than self-awareness. It is incredibly difficult to shine around these people, as they will constantly seek to put you down in order to make themselves feel better about themselves. It is unlikely that you will be able to count on them for support, as your achievements will make them feel even more insecure.

- They are constantly judging you. It is very difficult to speak openly and honestly with someone you feel is adjudicating your performance and just waiting to find something to criticise. Right now, you need someone who understands and appreciates you for who you are, not who they want you to be. I am sure you have a very well evolved self-critic, so you certainly don't need others around you to add to this evaluation burden. Trying to be 'good enough' for these people is an endless game.

- The caring and sharing is one-sided. Relationships are not a competition, but at the same time, a helpful relationship involves a mutual exchange of caring and sharing actions. There will be times when one person needs to help the other out of an emotional hole. But if you are always the one giving, listening or changing plans to make time to meet or share the realness of what is happening with you, then you may not be getting the level of respect and concern you need from the other person.

- You leave feeling physically and mentally drained. The lower levels of consciousness exert a very powerful and negative force, which brings you down and makes you feel physically sluggish and emotionally exhausted. Feelings such as shame, fear and anger trigger the release of stress hormones and kick off a set of physical reactions such as increased heart rate, sweaty palms, shallow breathing, muscle tension and nausea. If this is how you feel around a person, then it is a sure sign that their behaviour is triggering a stress response in you. This influence will limit your ability to think and act clearly and consciously.

Your Options for Unhelpful Relationships

What do you do with unhelpful relationships? You have a choice of taking five different actions when you realise that the relationship may be holding you back:

1. Nothing. That's right. The status quo is always an option. You may feel worried about insulting or hurting the other person, so you can decide not to say or do anything. Doing nothing may be appropriate if the relationship seems to be dwindling out naturally, or if you are making a move soon that will cause a distinct separation. But sometimes if you do decide to do nothing, you are choosing comfort over courage and therefore limiting your ability to move through to acceptance, love and joy.

2. Discuss your concerns. Now, this may make for a difficult conversation. Still, there are some wonderful assertive conversation techniques you can use to enable productive discussions. For example, if the other person is always interrupting, you can say, 'When you interrupt and don't let me finish, I feel frustrated and that you don't value my opinion. I would like you to let me complete my sentences and listen to my ideas before giving your own.' Assertive communication follows the template of: When you... I feel... I would like... The benefit of this approach is that their reaction will tell you whether the relationship is worth saving. They may apologise and actively attempt to change their behaviour to respect your opinion. Or they will not understand, come up with an excuse or use one of the behaviours above such as judging or criticising you for raising the issue.

3. Set boundaries. When someone belittles or criticises you, you always have the option of standing up for yourself by clearly and respectfully letting the other person know their comments are not appropriate or appreciated. If negative and unsupportive talk is bringing you down, then you can ask for this not to occur. Physically leaving is another way of setting boundaries, which shows that you are not willing to be around people that bring you down. You could also limit your interaction with this person just to social events so that you are not permitting their influence into your life to any great extent.

4. Detachment. When you cannot physically leave, detachment is always an option. This means that you disconnect yourself from the emotion of the situation and refuse to engage with the drama or negative behaviour. Detachment is best used as a short-term solution when you are trying to remain objective and not get sucked into a toxic situation. It is not a long-term solution and is best teamed with discussing your concerns or setting boundaries.

5. Release the relationship. When you have spent enough time with a person, you intuitively know whether they want the best for you or whether the relationship is holding you back. Of course, you may be afraid of insulting or hurting the other person. Still, if they are not supportive or uplifting, then your time and energy is better spent finding a community or relationship that can truly help you bloom.

'Never apologise for having high standards. People who really want to be in your life will rise up to meet them.'
~ Ziad K Abdelnour

What Supportive Relationships Look Like

In contrast, how do we know when we have the blessing of a supportive relationship? Often you feel it in your gut—your intuition tells you that you are in a safe and nurturing place. You feel comfortable and confident. Research shows that supportive relationships can create such a positive influence on your health and wellbeing that you live longer[26]. But how do you know a supportive relationship? What are the characteristics of a relationship that will help you bloom[27]?

1. They encourage self-acceptance and self-compassion. In contrast to unhelpful relationships where there is criticism and judgement, supportive relationships encourage you to love yourself through all of the highs and the lows. They want you to celebrate your successes and show self-compassion during times of challenge. They don't expect you to be perfect but want you to love and care for yourself just the way you are.

2. They keep you honest. Supportive relationships don't let us get away with behaviour that is going to hurt our integrity or end up again in places of fear or guilt. They hold us to high moral standards and keep us accountable to achieving our dreams. They dare to say what's on their mind and raise issues with you that are concerning them. They are careful not to hurt you but are also concerned to see you become the best person you can be.

3. They are present. Supportive people provide you with their full attention and awareness. They will certainly put away their phone to discuss important issues. They listen—really listen. They value your perspective, thoughts and ideas and validate your feelings. Supportive people ask lots of questions to understand your situation—how you are doing physically, mentally and emotionally—and how they can help.

4. They inspire you to be a better person. Supportive people keep us grounded and keep our egos in check when we are succeeding. They also see our amazing potential and encourage us when we fall to get back up and keep moving to realise it for ourselves. Supportive people provide an inspirational role model and, through their commitment to us, their kindness and persistence, they bring out the best in us.

Evaluate Your Current Network

Now you have some clear criteria for determining if a relationship you have with a person is either unhelpful or supportive. With this information, it is time for you to undertake an evaluation of how your current network may be helping or hindering your blooming.

Here is a summary table of characteristics to refer to:

Unhelpful relationships	Supportive Relationships
They are jealous	They encourage self-acceptance and self-compassion
They are constantly judging you	They keep you honest
The caring and sharing is one-sided	They are present
You leave physically and mentally drained	They inspire you to be a better person

Person /network	Unhelpful or supportive?	Why?	Action to take

Getting Your Team Ready

For a seed to sprout and grow, it relies on having many different factors working together in the right combination. The temperature, light, soil and water all have to be working in its favour. Your expedition is no different. You need a team of people who play different roles but are working together to achieve one great outcome: seeing you bloom.

Another way to think about it is that every day you head out into the world is like you are stepping into a sports arena. You are there to play the best game you can—to learn and to grow as a player and a person. But sportspeople don't just wander onto the field alone. They have had the benefit of a whole team around them getting them ready for this moment, who are there waiting to support them when the game is done. They have:

- Coaches;

- Teammates;

- Doctors; and

- Fans.

You need the same team in place to help you through the great adventure ahead.

Coaches

While there are days we might not want to hear it, we do need someone in our lives that will tell us the full and frank truth about our situation. This is the coach. They are there to give objective feedback and care enough about you to help you see the full picture. You may not like what they have to say, but you know it comes with a genuine and unwavering commitment to your flourishing. Coaches are the people that can help you question and change those things in your life that are not serving you. But it is not done out of jealousy or fear. It is done from a place of compassion and love. Coaches help you build courage to practise new skills and keep focused on the end goal of living up to your full potential. Without a coach on your team, you can lose direction, motivation or perspective about what is truly important.

Teammates

Teammates are people that are on the same journey as you and have great strengths that can help offset your weaknesses. You might be great at defensive play—that is, not letting negativity get you down. But your offensive game may be lacking. This is where a great teammate can help by giving you ideas and strategies to help move beyond the situation and find your best self. You might struggle with internal motivation, but a teammate might be all you need to get you up and out the door for that walk every morning. If your clothes are needing a make-over, then there just might be a teammate out there who knows all about clearing out the old when emotions to certain pieces are involved or who can help you no longer cover up in all black but find clothing that brings out your personalisation and highlights your beautiful body. Teammates fill the gaps in your skill sets, and the great thing is that you also do the same for them. Maybe you are the one that helps them see the silver lining in a challenging situation, or can teach them how to show compassion for themselves.

Doctors

Coaches and teammates play vital roles in our health and wellbeing. Still, there comes a time that you would also benefit from some further expertise, and this is where doctors are essential. When I say doctors, I don't just mean general practitioners or medical specialists that treat acute and chronic physical conditions. I also mean those practitioners that are there to keep you well and help you be your best. This may be on the physical side naturopaths, chiropractors, yoga instructors and massage therapists. In the mental and emotional arena, with psychologists, counsellors, meditation trainers or spiritual teachers. Practitioners have access to a range of diagnostic tools that may help you identify obstacles on your journey. They also have the knowledge and skills that can help you overcome them.

Fans

All along your expedition, you are going to need people to cheer you along. On the days that you don't think you can take another step, it can change your day to have someone on the sideline saying, 'Come on, you can do it.' Especially, on those days, we find it hard to believe in ourselves. We need fans to remind us of just how great we actually are. It's important to note that fans are not coaches. You won't get an objective analysis or honest opinion from a fan. That is not their role. For a fan, you can do wrong and they are the kind of people that will cheer you on no matter what direction you choose. Fans are essential to keep up your energy and momentum.

Who is on Your Team?

Previously you have evaluated those people or networks you currently have that are going to support your expedition to blooming. Cherish this list like your greatest prize, for truly helpful people are one of your best assets on this journey. Now it is time to determine what roles these people will play on your team.

Write down the list of supportive people or networks you have identified from the earlier exercise. Think about what role they play for you. Are they a coach, teammate, fan or doctor? You may also like to add some others here— that's totally okay too.

Supportive Person /network	Role	Why are they good at this role?

The next step is to identify if there are any imbalances or gaps in your team. While it would be wonderful to have a following of fans, that team is not going to help you critically evaluate your actions.

Review the roles you have identified as already having on your team and then determine:

- Are there any roles that appear to have too many on one team? Too many coaches may make life feel a bit serious and too much hard work. Too many teammates and you will never get to address any areas you need to develop, which are important for you to learn. Too many doctors and you begin to feel over-analysed and helpless. Too many fans and you will never have an honest opinion about how you can do better each day to be your best self.

- Are there any roles that appear to have too few on the team? Too few coaches and you may lose direction. Too few teammates and you may struggle to keep moving. Too few doctors and you may get lost in problems with no clear solution. Too few fans and the journey may start to feel long and hard. Are there any roles that would benefit you by having more of them on the team?

This is not to say that every one of these people or networks on your list is not valuable. The message is that you might need to make sure there is balance across the roles in order to have a high-performing team that will provide the right social environment for you to be able to bloom and nurture your seed. So, if you find you have too many of a particular role, see if you can balance this out by adding more to other roles or spending more time with the other roles in your team. This will help you get a fuller perspective and a holistic blend of care and support. If you don't have any people in a particular role or have too few, then you may want to consider finding some more people to play this role for you. Believe it or not, so many people are on the same journey as you, and with the passion and desire to help you too. You just have to take action to find them.

Where to Find Your Team

If you are just starting your expedition, it can feel like you are all alone. This is especially the case if you are walking away from negative thought patterns and behaviours that were unhelpful, but which you have known for years. You are moving forward and so will need to establish networks that reflect where you want to be, not where you are now. So, where do you find this team? I think you may be surprised that when you start practising the skills of self-acceptance and self-compassion, many new people may come into your life. Your energy will shift, and people who feel the same way will be drawn to you, and you to them. Finding your tribe, your team, is a process of evolution, but this does take time. So, to get your start with support right now, there are some places you can go to seek out like-minded people for your team:

- Volunteering—do you have a social cause you are passionate about? It might be helping sick kids, the elderly or the homeless. There are so many non-profit groups out there that would love your passion and assistance. In addition to doing great work, you will get to meet like-minded people, have meaningful conversations and begin to broaden your community.

- Meet-up groups—there may be meet-up groups run by people who are passionate about the same things as you. You can meet up with others that share your love of cinema, vegan cooking or ninja courses. You will see that the possibilities are endless. All it takes is the courage to pick one, and the commitment to turn up and give it a go.

- Fitness groups—if you are starting a new fitness adventure, it would be very wise to learn from people who have been through the same challenges. Finding people that are already doing what you want to do is a sure-fire way to success. They are a ready source of coaches, teammates and fans and, before you know it, you could have a new member on your support team.

- Social media—for all of its cautions, social media does provide a place where you can find people for your team or networks to join. Seek out people and groups on social media, and trust your instincts. You can start by looking up certain hashtags or geo locations and sending a simple message to say 'hi'. You'll instantly know if the other person has some of the same value sets as you. For example, do they love to use emojis? Do they ask questions back? Are they receptive and responsive to your messages? What energy do you feel is being received? Even try getting into voice messaging—remembering that you are taking on courage.

WHAT NEXT?

Your social environment can make or break your expedition. The people around you can make this journey feel like an exciting adventure or the greatest battle of your life. The good news is that you get to create your own team and can take action today to get the right people to support and cheer you on and the not right fit for now people released from your team. There are things you can do that will lessen the influence of unhelpful people in your life and increase the influence of supportive and nurturing friends. You can work to build a team that will sustain you on your path.

'Self-reliance is the only road to true freedom,
and being one's own person is its ultimate reward.'
~ Patricia Sampson

Ultimately, though, you are responsible for your future and the actions that you take. No-one else is going to take care of you. You have to do this for yourself. That is why the next chapters will remind you of the power you have to support your own body, mind and seed (spirit). Sometimes there is no-one else around to help. So, the following chapters will remind you that you are and will always be the most valuable player on your team!

COMMITMENT STATEMENT

I commit to surrounding myself with people
who will bring positivity into my life and who
will help me grow and bloom into the
best person I can be.

CHAPTER FIFTEEN

Caring for Your Body

'Beauty is being the best possible version
of yourself, inside and out.'
~ Audrey Hepburn

Blooming from the Inside Out

You may remember, in the very first chapter, we discussed the two key roles our body plays, these being:

1. As a way we interact with the world; and

2. As a home for our unique spirit (seed).

Caring for your body means recognising and respecting both of these roles, and keeping them in balance. For when we place too much focus on how others see our body, then we can get lost in the mire of self-consciousness. When we are preoccupied with our body and what other people think about it, we lose the ability to listen. We become too distracted to wholly engage with the other person and form meaningful relationships. Likewise, though, if we neglect this role—if we don't care for our own needs—then it is likely there won't be many people that would care to spend time with us either. How we care for our bodies sends a clear signal to the world about the level of respect and love we have for ourselves.

So, while the two roles have equal importance, it is really only possible to bloom from the inside out. For it is the awareness, courage and compassion we have for ourselves that influences our mood, our posture and the energy that we send out into the world. We can lather ourselves with makeup and invest in body-sculpting underwear but the reality is that this will not make you feel comfortable or confident in your own skin for the long term. Without the inner work on self-acceptance and compassion, the façade may look great but the foundations are shaky. Other people sense how comfortable you are in your own skin as well. Your level of self-acceptance will rub off on them. You will find that people really enjoy being around you when you have a sense of security and ease in yourself. That is why recognising our inner beauty must come first. Because this will allow us to enact the second role—moving forward in the world with ease and confidence, which allows us to share our unique gifts.

Caring for Your Body from the Inside Out

It is no surprise that how we take care of our internal physical health has significant ramifications for our external appearance. What we eat directly affects the quality of our skin. Lack of sleep creates dark circles under the eyes. The amount and type of exercise we do shows in our muscle tone and posture. All of these aspects of physical health also have substantial impacts on our mental wellbeing too. There will be many challenges on your journey to blooming, and being strong in body and mind will give you the best chance of working through them. In the next chapters, we will focus on how to care for your thoughts and feelings, but for now, let's see how you nourish the seed within to grow and bloom.

Nutrition

'Tell me what you eat, and I will tell you what you are.'
~ Anthelme Brillat-Savarin

One of the breakthrough moments for me in my body battles came when I learned the basics of nutrition. I realised that the food and drink we choose to consume can either be our greatest help or our most toxic hindrance. Some of the foods we eat can provide incredible vitality, create life and energy and leave us feeling great. Other foods can sap our energy, dampen our moods and leave us feeling dull and lifeless.

I am going to be clear right now, though, that in my opinion there are no 'right' or 'wrong' foods. Categorising foods so simply is impossible. Even a can of Coke can be life-giving for a person just rescued from the desert (although water would be a better option!). If you were to ask me what food is better, broccoli or chocolate cake, I would need to ask you first about the context. Are you stuck on the bottom of a mountain with no option but to climb? Or are you sitting down to your normal evening meal? Of course, if you have to climb a mountain, the chocolate cake is a no-brainer. You are going to need its condensed energy to spur you on to the challenges ahead. A bowl of broccoli is not going to get you very far. I suspect halfway up you would have been wishing you chose the chocolate cake! What is right will depend on the context of the situation and your own personal nutritional needs.

The first consideration with regards to context is your energy needs for the day. Food is the greatest source of fuel for our bodies and minds, and it provides this energy in three ways:

1. Regularity of intake. Food is converted to glucose in our bodies, which is used as a great source of energy. Around five hours after you eat, the amount of glucose in your blood drops. If not restored, you can get all kinds of symptoms of low blood sugar such as brain fog, weakness, shakiness, irritability or headaches. This certainly does not lead to good decision-making, and your journey to bloom needs the clearest attention and best decisions you can make.

2. Quantity consumed. Having a consistent level of energy throughout the day is as simple as balancing the amount of energy you consume with the amount of energy you expend. Think about it like a bucket with a hole in it. The amount of energy you put in from eating and drinking leaks out based on the amount of energy you expend. If you balance energy in with energy out, everything stays stable. Not having enough energy

in the bucket can impact on motivation, mood and your ability to think clearly. Likewise, putting greater amounts of energy into the bucket than is going out creates a flood or block of energy. It creates pressure on your digestive organs such as the liver and stomach that need to digest and help move through all of the food. Under-consumption can leave you feeling lethargic because of a lack of fuel. Over-consumption creates stress and exhaustion because of the additional digestive burden on the body.

3. Quality of food and drink. Have you heard of the saying, 'Garbage in, garbage out'? This is exactly the situation when it comes to nutrition. As I have said before, every food has an appropriate context, but use it in the wrong context and you can be in a world of danger. For example, processed foods are handy if you are out camping or don't have access to refrigeration equipment for fresh food. They have a very important place, but it is certainly not in every meal. The additives, preservatives, colourings and flavourings put into processed foods tend to be synthetic and your liver needs to process all of them. Their harmful side effects are well known for anyone with allergies to them. But even if we don't have an acute reaction, there is no doubt in my mind that the further a food is away from nature, the harder it is for our body to digest. In turn, this creates more burden for our body and lowers our energy, as the digestive organs are slowed and burdened by the extra work involved.

Moreover, research has shown that what we eat and drink affects the health of our gut. Our gut manages numerous neurotransmitters in the brain, and these influence our emotions and our ability to deal with stress and pain. Put in food that fosters gut health, and we can become more courageous. Input food that destroys gut health, and we can become more angry and fearful. The foods and drinks you choose to consume are either working for or against your mission to bloom.

The message then when it comes to nutrition is to stop and think before you prepare or buy a meal, specifically about:

- What you need; and

- How you want to feel after you eat it.

Do you need a meal that is going to provide you with vitamins, minerals, proteins, fibre and sustained energy for your day? Do you want a meal that will help you feel mentally clear, calm and physically balanced? Or do you need a calorie-dense snack to power you up that mountain? Remember, too much or too little food can be problematic, but so can choosing food that is against what your body needs at the time. Respect your body and give it what it needs so that it can support you to be your very best every day.

Sleep

I truly feel for those of you who have sleep problems such as insomnia or apnoea. I know for myself just how one rough night's sleep disturbs the whole next day, let alone also a month. I know first hand how debilitating it is to have this continue night after night. Living your life tired makes even the smallest worries seem huge, and saps your energy and optimism. Why is this the case? Why is sleep so important?

The latest research has found that sleep is the only time that the brain gets cleaned. In other parts of our body, we have lymph glands that remove toxins, but the brain has no such mechanism. So, when we sleep, the brain shrinks ever so slightly, and the liquid surrounding the brain (cerebrospinal fluid or CSF) washes through and over it[28]. If you don't get a good night's sleep, the wastes and 'toxins' don't get cleared from your brain. That is why you feel so dull and hazy when you are tired! You can think of your brain like a car wash.

You wouldn't drive out halfway through the cycle with dirt and soap left on to ruin your polish. In the same way, you would want to ensure that the brain gets a full clean before you head out for another busy day.

A good night's sleep is important to provide:

- Clarity of thought to deal with daily challenges and make decisions that serve us well; and

- Physical strength to move through the day with confidence and hope.

The good news is that many of the things that help with a great night's sleep are completely within our control. It is just up to us to take responsibility for our health and wellbeing and put tomorrow's wellbeing ahead of tonight's enjoyment! For example, the list of 'don't dos' before bed includes:

- Don't drink caffeine, alcohol or have excessive fluids before bed as they can induce stimulation or change your natural sleep rhythm.

- Limit screen time, especially before bedtime. The blue light impacts on the production of melatonin, which helps regulate our sleep cycle.

- Avoid long naps during the day or keep them to less than 40 minutes.

- Limit your stress and worry before bed. I know this is easier said than done, but stress and worry impacts on both the quality and quantity of sleep.

The list of things that you can do to encourage a great night's sleep include:

- Have a consistent time for going to bed and waking, and keep these the same even on the weekends and holidays.

- Use a bedtime routine to create a sense of peace and calm. Dimming the lights, taking a warm bath, turning on relaxing music, reading or meditation are all great options to set the scene for sleep.

- Increase physical activity during the day. As exercise is a short-term stimulant, if it is done too close to bedtime it can interrupt the ability to get to sleep (during the day it can aid in sleep ~ pretty great hey?!).

Sleep can be one of your greatest allies on your expedition if you treat it with the respect that it deserves. It is there to keep us mentally and physically charged for the exciting adventures ahead. If you find yourself struggling physically or mentally throughout the day, then taking a look at your sleep habits is a great place to start.

Breathing

'Breathe in deeply to bring your mind
home to your body.'
~ Thich Nhat Hanh

I describe our breath as our best friend, one that is always with us to nurture and support us. It is truly an ally on your journey to blooming as it energises and motivates you to take action, but can also ground and calm you in times of distress.

Our bodies use the oxygen we breathe in to produce energy from what we eat. This process is called cellular respiration. The cells in our body need oxygen to break down sugars from our food into energy our body can use. This energy is either used immediately or stored in the cells for future energy needs. So if you are not breathing properly and getting enough oxygen in the body, the cells would find it difficult to produce enough energy. Insufficient oxygen intake is associated with mental and physical fatigue. This is why the breath is so essential on your expedition. It will help fuel the positive mindset and physical state you need to take action and overcome obstacles along the way. It is difficult to bloom when all you feel like doing is wilting.

Breathing also has other incredibly important impacts on both physical and mental wellbeing. Research[29] has shown that deep breathing exercises actually trigger the parasympathetic nervous system, which is the relaxation system of the body. This, in turn, can help reduce the physical responses you may feel when operating at the lower levels of consciousness. When you are experiencing fear, anger, guilt or shame, your body and mind can have the following reactions:

- Increased heart rate;

- Increased blood pressure;

- Muscle tension; and

- Decreased ability to think and concentrate.

However, by reconnecting with your best friend, the breath, you can counter these distressing physiological effects and return yourself to a place where you can think clearly and take actions that care for yourself and those around you.

But don't take my word for it. Try this simple three-part deep breathing exercise and see how you feel afterwards.

- Inhale:
    1. Breathe in through your nose and fill up your belly like a balloon.
    2. Fill your rib cage; feel each and every space between the ribs become wider.
    3. Finish by filling up your upper chest.

- Exhale:
    1. Release the breath through your nose from your chest.
    2. Feel your rib cage become tighter, and the spaces between the ribs become smaller.
    3. Use your abdominal muscles to push out any stagnant air at the bottom of your belly.

Move through the process slowly to get familiar with it. Start with about 10–15 breaths and work your way up to 20–25 breaths in one session.

'Breathe deeply, until sweet air extinguishes the burn of
fear in your lungs, and every breath is a beautiful refusal to
become anything less than infinite.'

~ D. Antoinette Foy

Exercise

I have talked to many people about exercise, and it seems that there are two kinds of people: those who love it and those who hate it. Interestingly, those who love it now do admit to disliking it in the beginning. It was a lot of hard work until they built up a level of fitness where they can now really enjoy it. Those who hate it are either at the beginning of their journey or are the kinds of people who are just not ready to challenge themselves or grow physically, mentally or spiritually. And if you are anything like me, exercise wasn't a priority growing up, so was rarely an activity I grew up doing.

The thing is, there are so many forms of exercise. And when I say the word 'exercise', I know we tend to think of some of the more monotonous forms like running, swimming laps or a cycle class at the gym. But what about team sports—exercise with a social element as well? What about a hike in the wilderness? What about paddle-boarding on the ocean? Truly, the most important question is not 'what' exercise you are doing, but 'why' you are doing it.

Exercising because of fear, shame, guilt or pride might get you up and moving in the short term, but it is not going to provide long-term motivation. Understanding *why* exercise is important and beneficial for your body, mind and seed will provide the inspiration to sustain it as part of your lifestyle.

So, why is exercise a wise choice? Scientific studies show that physical activity has direct positive effects on both the structure and the function of our muscles, hearts and brains. It also affects our intellect, mood and overall wellbeing. Specifically related to your *Body Beautiful* journey, exercise:

- Helps process and regulate emotions such as fear and anger;

- Boosts your energy and mood to take positive action; and

- Improves memory, focus and attention.

During and after exercise, there are a whole host of chemical reactions that take place in your body and mind. Neurotransmitters such as serotonin, norepinephrine and dopamine are released. These help with information processing, motivation, energy and concentration. At the same time, depending on your level of physical activity, this can help to decrease the levels of cortisol and adrenaline in the body, which are stress hormones. The reduction in stress hormones and the increase in happy hormones is the reason you get the 'feel-good' sensations after you exercise.

The added benefit of exercise is that it can also provide secondary benefits that are important for you. For example, joining a walking group or local sporting club provides social connections. Yoga or tai chi provides relaxation and perhaps spiritual intrigue as well. Signing up for a triathlon or ninja warrior course will deliver a great sense of personal challenge and achievement. With our busy schedules, it is a clever strategy to choose an exercise that ticks a few important boxes and, these days, the options available to you are absolutely endless. Exercise will help you be physically strong, mentally clear, emotionally positive and spiritually inspired.

The Wisdom of Our Bodies

Our bodies are more than just a mass of tissue and bone. They hold so much wisdom that, if we are willing to listen closely, we can tap into. When we feel emotions, a whole range of chemical reactions are triggered in the brain. This causes a wave of other reactions right through our body so that our mental and spiritual states become full-body experiences. For example, when someone gives you a compliment, the ventral striatum area of the brain lights up. Interestingly, this is the same area that is activated when we receive money. Then the neurotransmitter dopamine is released, which creates feelings of positivity and motivation. However, so many of our emotions go unnoticed. If we can listen carefully to our bodies, then we can more fully understand what is going on for us in any moment, and care for our thoughts and feelings that are present.

Bringing Consciousness to Body Care

The first step to making positive change in our lives is always becoming aware of not only what we are doing, but also what is driving those actions. That is, what beliefs, thoughts or feelings are driving us to behave a certain way. While we may understand the benefits of nutrition, sleep and exercise theoretically, when it comes to embedding these things in our lives, we may find ourselves sabotaging our efforts and giving up. But why? Well, if you truly believe that you do not deserve to be confident and fully bloom, then no matter how much you profess and dream of the possibilities ahead, your mind will find a way to sabotage your efforts. This is why The Retreat is an essential first step of your journey to blooming, because we need to understand and care for ourselves in order to challenge our limiting beliefs and support ourselves to make positive changes to our lives and to bloom.

Are you committed to sharing your unique beauty with this world? Are you committed to living your best life and letting your beauty bloom? Then stepping out into the world requires you to care for yourself as best as you can, every day. To do this, take some time to reflect on how conscious and caring you are for each of the vital health elements we just covered. Also, use this opportunity to dig deep and see if there are any limiting beliefs holding you back in this area.

	How many stars would you give yourself?			
	How much awareness do you bring to this element each day?	How much care do you give in this area?	Are there any beliefs holding you back in this area?	Are there any actions that you could take to improve your physical health?
Nutrition	★ ★ ★ ★ ★	★ ★ ★ ★ ★	★ ★ ★ ★ ★	★ ★ ★ ★ ★
Sleep	★ ★ ★ ★ ★	★ ★ ★ ★ ★	★ ★ ★ ★ ★	★ ★ ★ ★ ★
Breath	★ ★ ★ ★ ★	★ ★ ★ ★ ★	★ ★ ★ ★ ★	★ ★ ★ ★ ★
Exercise	★ ★ ★ ★ ★	★ ★ ★ ★ ★	★ ★ ★ ★ ★	★ ★ ★ ★ ★

WHAT NEXT?

Caring for your body is the ultimate act of self-respect. Providing yourself care gives you the energy to be the best you can be that day but is also caring for your future self. Eating, exercising, sleeping and breathing well are the acts of care that your future self will thank you for. Because our body and mind are carefully connected, caring for your body will naturally deliver benefits for your thoughts and overall mindset. One feeds the other and vice versa.

However, no matter how well we nourish our bodies, we will always encounter difficult thoughts. We have seen how embedded our limiting beliefs can be. As long as they exist, regardless of how small they are, they can create negative and unhelpful actions. So knowing how to deal with negative and unhelpful thoughts is essential. Without these skills, we are in danger of sabotaging our development and giving up on our expedition. Your potential is far too precious to let thoughts get in the way, so let's find out how to interrupt the influence of thoughts that threaten to interrupt your journey.

COMMITMENT STATEMENT

I commit to caring for my body by providing nourishing food and making time for exercise in my day. I commit to supporting myself to bloom by bringing awareness to my breath and providing sufficient sleep to rest and renew.

CHAPTER SIXTEEN

Caring for Your Thoughts

'The most decisive event in your life comes when you discover
you are not your thoughts.'

~ Eckhart Tolle

What Are Thoughts?

Right now, reading this book, you are having so many thoughts. But have you ever stopped to think exactly what thoughts are and where they come from? Have you ever contemplated what role they play in your life? Well, if you are like most people, you are not even aware of most of the thoughts you have each day. There are different opinions on this number, but on average, it is estimated that we have around 50,000 thoughts a day. This equates to 2000 thoughts every hour of the day. Or, if you take the time off for sleep, then you are having around 3000 thoughts every waking hour. This is incredible! No wonder we feel overwhelmed sometimes.

At their most basic, thoughts are just the reaction between electrical impulses and chemicals in the brain[30]. We become aware of thoughts when a message from one neuron is received by another neuron. As we have heard in the previous chapter, our body is a complex system. There are thousands of messages being sent throughout the day to maintain our physical health. We have thoughts to let us know we are hungry, too hot, too cold, or whether we feel safe or threatened.

But we also have a huge number of thoughts that are driven by our beliefs. Remember The Self-Fulfilling Action Cycle from Chapter 6? This showed us that when we have helpful and positive beliefs about ourselves and the world, these will naturally bring forth thoughts that are grounded in acceptance, joy and love. However, if we have beliefs that are negative or unhelpful, then, without intervention of some kind, these will likely result in thoughts grounded in fear, guilt or anger.

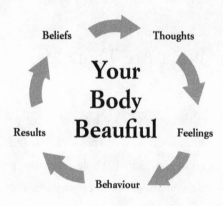

Figure 28 – The Self-Fulfilling Action Cycle

The Influence of Thoughts

What is even more important than the occurrence of thoughts is the influence that they can have over our lives. As shown in the diagram above, while thoughts are driven by our beliefs, they can set off a whole chain reaction of events. They prompt feelings, which can lead us to take actions, all of which have outcomes or consequences. Actions driven by the higher levels of consciousness have results that power us towards acceptance, joy and love. On the other hand, actions driven by the lower levels of consciousness result in the forces of fear, guilt, anger, grief and shame.

So just like a ripple, thoughts can send big waves throughout our lives. But here is the key point. Thoughts have no power by themselves. They are only electrical signals. We give them power by allowing ourselves to get hooked by them.

Getting Hooked by Your Thoughts

Let me show you the power of getting hooked by your thoughts with a simple exercise. For each of the following scenarios, write down the first thought that shows up in your mind.

Scenario	Your first thought
You catch sight of yourself naked in the mirror.	
Someone tells you that you have put on weight.	
You see an advertisement for a revolutionary new cellulite treatment.	
Swimsuits only now come as a thong bikini.	

Look over the list of thoughts you had. How many of them began with or included the following statements:

- I should

- I should not

- I must

- I must not

- I have to

- I always

- I never

- I can't

These thought patterns are restrictive and do not serve you at all in your expedition to bloom. They spark emotions of shame, fear, guilt and anger and keep you in the lower levels of consciousness. They reflect three unhelpful ways of thinking:

1. Rigid expectations—When we have hard ideas about how we should be, we are less accepting and compassionate towards ourselves and others. Examples include, 'I shouldn't be feeling this way,' 'They should be kind,' or 'It needs to be perfect.'

2. Judgements—When we judge things by black or white categories such as good or bad, fair or unfair, right and wrong, we cause a great deal of internal conflict. We lose acceptance for ourselves and get caught up in the way we want things to be, rather than the way things are and we don't see other possibilities.

3. Self-focused fusion—When we hook into unhelpful self-descriptions or identities. For example, 'I am weak,' 'I am the ugly one,' or 'I don't need help.'

Now, look over your list of thoughts. Where you used unhelpful hooks, change the sentences to start with one of the following:

- I will

- I decide

- I choose

- I want to

- I choose not to

Do you see how this simple change in words brings a whole new perspective to your thoughts? Instead of being brought down by the negative forces of expectation and judgement, you are lifted up by using your own power in this world to choose and decide what is right for you. Reframing your thoughts turns you from a victim to a creator of your own life and your future.

How You Deal with Uncomfortable Thoughts

The danger with unhelpful thoughts is if they create action that is both automatic and destructive to your wellbeing. We all have myriad ways that we deal with the discomfort that difficult thoughts and feelings can bring. These include:

- Distracting ourselves from painful thoughts. For example, by watching television, sleeping or reading.

- Opting out of activities. For example, not going to parties or social events.

- Doing more thinking to find a logical way out of the thought. For example, analysing, imagining, worrying or blaming.

- Numbing out. For example, using substances such as alcohol or binge eating.

You may not even realise you are doing these things because our reactions to uncomfortable thoughts are largely hardwired in our brain. We tend to respond the same way over and over again, and if the response works to provide some relief or short-term satisfaction, then we just keep doing it. You never get to address the unhelpful thought that you are having about yourself and keep continuing the cycle that is ultimately not serving you to bloom. While such responses are convenient short-term solutions, if they continue, they end up becoming a concern and problem of the bigger issue that's not growing—your self-confidence.

Caring for Your Thoughts

If you haven't noticed by now, you can't control your thoughts. In fact, the more you try to stop thoughts coming, the harder they resist and they just come back bigger and more often. Instead of trying to push thoughts away, there is an alternative action that is much kinder and more compassionate towards yourself: creating a space between the thought and action. This allows you to assess if you are getting hooked and provides the time for you to decide what the next best action could be.

Caring for your thoughts is a three-step process that I know called 'Notice, Name and Tame'[31]:

1. Notice: This is where self-awareness shines. When you can step into the observing self, you can see objectively what thoughts are arising. You can notice the thoughts for just what they are—only thoughts.

2. Name: To give yourself some distance from the thoughts, it is effective to name them using the words:

    'I am having the thought that…'

    This allows you to keep the thought in perspective and creates some distance to prevent you from getting hooked by it.

3. Tame: There are two great techniques you can use to quieten the

thoughts that arise and persist. The first is a simple question. You can ask yourself whether this thought is helpful or whether this thought will help you bloom. The second is the Decision-Making Matrix, which helps you determine whether you do need to take any action from the thought. Whether you need to take action depends on how important the issue is to you, and the amount of influence or control you have over the situation.

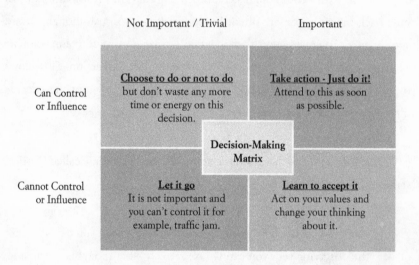

Figure 29 – The Decision-Making Matrix

Sometimes you don't realise you are hooked until you are hours into rumination and worry or deep down the chip packet or ice-cream tub. Becoming aware of our thoughts—being able to notice them and name them—takes practise, but the rewards are definitely worthwhile. Being able to care for and manage your thoughts frees up so much energy in your day, and makes sure the actions you are taking are directed towards making peace with your body and being your own best friend. You may not be able to control your thoughts, but if you don't become aware of and care for your thoughts, they will certainly control you now and determine your future.

What Caring for Your Thoughts Looks Like

Let's work through an example to show what the process of noticing, naming and taming your thoughts looks like. We will use the example we worked through in Chapter 7 of the woman who was invited to the beach by her friends. Let's call her Alice. You might remember the situation was framed by the following:

- Belief—Alice believes she looks ugly in a swimsuit. She constantly looks at herself in the mirror, wearing the latest style, and feels embarrassed.

- Thoughts—When Alice receives an invitation to go to the beach with friends, she immediately thinks that she won't swim because people will judge and make fun of her.

These thoughts resulted in her feeling sad, not swimming and missing out on the things in life she truly loves. It is highly likely that when Alice received the invitation, the more specific thoughts that popped into her head were things like:

- I should go on that diet;

- I should not be seen in a swimsuit; and

- I can't go swimming.

Usually, when these kinds of thoughts arise, Alice distracts herself by sitting in front of the television and binge-watching the latest series on Netflix. But what happens if, right then, Alice becomes aware of these thoughts and begins the steps of caring for them? She sits on her bed and has the following conversation with herself:

'I am having the thought that I look ugly in a swimsuit and that I can't go swimming with my friends.'

'I am worried that people might laugh at me and then I will end up feeling ashamed of who I am.'

'This thought is not helpful to me living my best life.'

'My body shape is important to me but, right now, I cannot control it, so I will let it go and live by my values.'

'Right now, what is most important to me is swimming in the ocean, connecting with nature and sharing great experiences with my friends. I have control over being able to do these things now.'

'So, I choose to acknowledge my discomfort about being in a swimsuit in public, but I choose not to let it stop me from enjoying my life. I will go and have fun, laugh and enjoy the sunshine. This will help me be my best self.'

Good on Alice! I know I hear you thinking this too. We know that by Alice bringing awareness to her thoughts and treating them with care, she has moved from unconscious harmful actions to conscious and compassionate behaviour. By interrupting the chain of thoughts, feelings and actions, she has empowered herself to choose actions that support her best life, things she enjoys and supporting the sprouting of her blooming for the unique beauty that's always resided in her.

Now it is Your Turn

As you go about your day, see if you can notice any thoughts as they arise. They may be helpful or disturbing. The key is to just begin to become aware of your thoughts. It does not matter if you only notice you were trapped in a thought several hours later. Congratulate yourself at any time you notice your thoughts, because awareness is the first and most important step of living consciously and confidently in your own skin.

When you become aware of the thought, practise naming it. Try using the words, 'I am having the thought that…' and see if that works for you to help keep the thought in perspective as only a thought and not actually who you are.

Then tame the thought by:

- Checking whether the thought is helpful; or
- Using the Decision-Making Matrix in Figure 30 to determine whether any action needs to be taken.

Here is a template that may be helpful for you to work through this process.

I am having the thought that...	Is this thought helpful? Yes/No	How important is this issue to me? (High, Medium or Low)	How much control do I have over this issue? (High, Medium or Low)	Is there any action I need to take on this thought? Yes/No. If so, what action?

Like mastering any new skill, caring for your thoughts takes practise. Remember to be kind to yourself. Congratulate yourself whenever you become aware of a thought. Know that by bringing awareness to your thoughts, you are one step closer to supporting your future self, who is at peace with her body and allowing herself to bloom.

WHAT NEXT?

We have seen the influential role that thoughts play in our lives, and the ability they have to control our feelings and actions if we let them go unchecked. It is important to remember that thoughts do not define us. Thoughts may be a part of us, but they are not us. They will come and go, as we have seen thousands of times a day. We determine how much power we give them by letting them hook into us.

The bridge between our thoughts and actions are feelings, and this is the next stage of the Action Cycle where our expedition can derail. Emotions can motivate and inspire us to be our best. But they can also drag us down to the depths of despair. Being a whole person and living a full life means embracing both of these sides of life—the positive and negative. However, the same rule applies for feelings as it does for thoughts: when we bring awareness to them and care for them, we can transform our lives and our future. Feelings have a great deal of wisdom we can tap into, if only we take the time to stop and listen. In the next chapter, I will show you how to listen to your feelings and the messages that they may be sending you. In the meantime, though, remember to keep practising becoming aware of your thoughts. This skill will serve you well.

COMMITMENT STATEMENT

I commit to remembering that my thoughts do not define me. I commit to becoming aware of them, letting go of those that are not helpful and caring for those that can help me grow and bloom.

CHAPTER SEVENTEEN

Caring for Your Emotions

'Feelings are much like waves, we can't stop them from coming, but we can choose which ones to surf.' ~ Jonatan Mårtensson

---

What Are Emotions?

There are numerous theories about what emotions actually are, ranging from the scientific to the metaphysical and esoteric. Nevertheless, there is agreement about the three key aspects of emotions[32], being:

1. An experience—an internal or external trigger;

2. A physiological reaction—a reaction in the mind and body; and

3. A behavioural response—the physiological state is expressed, or some action is taken.

When shown visually, the way these aspects work together make one thing very clear: emotions are a flow—a movement of energy.

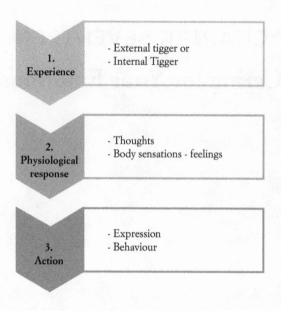

Figure 30 – The Three Elements of Emotions

When you break down the word 'emotion', you get 'e-motion' or energy in motion[33], which is exactly what we see. Energy comes to us in the thoughts of external stimuli or internal states. The energy gets transformed into internal thoughts and sensations in our body (feelings). Then the energy flows outwards in terms of us showing some expression or taking action in response to the thoughts and emotions we are having.

Let's continue working with Alice to see how this plays out. The trigger for Alice's original situation was both external and internal. The external trigger was the invitation from her friends to go to the beach. The internal trigger was the belief that she looks ugly in a swimsuit. These triggers set off a chain of physiological events in Alice. First, she begins thinking that she can't go swimming and how much fun she will miss out on. Now, if she lets these thoughts continue, they will flow on to feelings—physical sensations in Alice's body—that we might call sadness. She may feel a heaviness in her heart, a constriction in her throat and tears in her eyes. Then comes the action. In this case for Alice, it is a text message back to her friends that she will come to the beach but won't be swimming, with the ultimate consequence of her missing out on so much joy and connection.

Emotions Are Like Waves

Speaking of a trip to the beach, you can imagine that emotions are really like waves. They come into our bodies and flow outwards. But just like waves in the ocean, they come in all shapes and sizes. Some are small little ripples that pass through us quickly and are hardly noticed. Others appear like large tsunamis that seem to hold us down for days, months or even years. How long have you found yourself drowning in a deluge of sadness, fear or shame?

Research has shown that the duration of an emotion is, at the very longest, just 90 seconds[34]. Isn't that incredible! Each feeling we have is actually a chemical process that happens in the body and takes only 1.5 minutes. But hang on, what about the tsunamis we feel? How does the 90 second theory work for those emotions that either lift us up or bring us down for days or even years? There are two explanations for this:

1. What we are experiencing is actually a lot of little waves of emotion

at close intervals. We are just not aware enough to notice the space between when one wave ceases and another begins.

2. After 90 seconds, the chemical reaction of the emotion—the transference to thoughts and feelings—passes. Still, we may choose to stay in an unhelpful cognitive loop. A cognitive loop is when you have a thought reaction to your feelings, which just keeps bringing about more feelings, and the thought/feeling cycle goes on and on and on. Here is Alice's example of a cognitive loop.

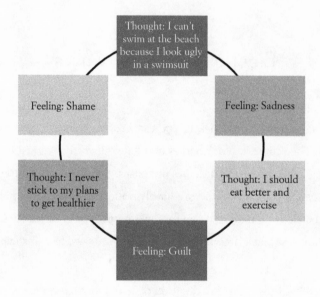

Figure 31 – Staying Under the Wave: A Cognitive Loop

Notice how the thoughts keeping Alice stuck in this loop are those unhelpful ones we covered in the previous chapter. That is, those using the words 'should', 'must', 'never' and 'can't'. If we allow our unhelpful thoughts to keep churning up unhelpful emotions, then we are allowing ourselves to stay trapped under the wave. Anyone else need a snorkel right now? Me too!

The Dangers of Denial or Repression

The other unhelpful reaction to emotions is when we try to deny their existence or stop them from coming altogether. I can only speak for my own situation, but my parents were never taught about emotions or how to care for them. They were very much taught that they just got in the way of work and, in fact, were a sign of weakness. Remaining emotionless at all times was expected. Crying, yelling, laughing too loud or dancing with joy were not appreciated. It is understandable that if our parents were not raised to recognise and respect their emotions, then they would not have taught us how to care for them when we were growing up.

Denial or repression were the key responses to emotions in my youth. The results were obvious. There would be annual outbursts of anger that had built up so much they could no longer be held back. There was loneliness and isolation with sadness and joy that was never validated or shared. There were mental and physical ramifications from the grief that was ignored.

When you think about it, denying your emotions is like pretending the wave is not there. You can turn your back on it, but it is still going to hit you. You can tell yourself the wave doesn't exist, but it will still soak you. Ignoring the existence of the wave does not make it go away; it just inhibits your ability to get the important messages that the emotion is sending. It is like spending the day standing in the waves and then hopping back in the car drenched— but ignoring the fact that you're soaking wet. Then heading to a restaurant still wet, but trying to ignore the fact. Then going to bed, yes, still wet, but just pretending you're not. The wave has done its work. It has an impact, and to deny it is completely nonsensical. This is like the people you meet who have anger written all over their faces. But when you ask them what is wrong they say, 'Nothing, I'm fine,' through gritted teeth. The emotion is obvious to everyone else, and denying it is not being honest with yourself or others.

Repressing your emotions is just as destructive. It is like putting up a big wall to block the waves. The waves are still pounding on the other side, but their effect is being obstructed by your wall of repression. There is just one important fact being missed from this approach. The waves will keep crashing and pounding and will one day wear down your wall. With all that water built up on the other side, there will inevitably be a flood. Because you have not learned to deal with the waves as they came along before, you are certainly very unprepared to deal with a tidal wave. This is what has happened when people have an outburst or 'snap'. Their wall has broken, and they will need a lot of assistance to deal with the carnage of so many repressed emotions.

Are There Good and Bad Emotions?

I am sure you are thinking though that some emotions are bad, that they are extremely distressing and therefore should be ignored or repressed. Just think about the definition of emotions, though—they are energy in motion. They are a bunch of chemical and physical reactions throughout the body and mind. Therefore, they are neither good nor bad. No emotion is either right or wrong. They just are flows of energy, waves of emotion that are passing through you in response to an experience. Most likely, this response is caused by an attachment to a thought or a story from your past experience. We encounter a situation that is like one from the past, so our automatic pilot kicks in and we re-enact old events and stories that are no longer relevant and no longer serve us.

Just as there are primary colours that are mixed to make other colours, the latest research shows that there are just four basic emotions that mix to make all the other emotions[35]. These primary or core emotions are:

- Anger

- Fear

- Sadness

- Happiness

When you feel an emotion such as shame, what you are feeling is a blend of both fear and sadness. You are afraid of the standards of yourself or others and are saddened by the prospect of not being able to fulfil them. When you feel bored, you may be feeling a blend of anger and fear. You are angry that your time is not being better used, but are afraid of seeking something that can challenge you. Wow, feelings are complex, aren't they?

Each one of these feelings also has a range of intensity, going from mild to moderate expressions, all the way through to dramatic intensities. For example, anger can manifest in a mild form as upset, tension or irritation. In its moderate form, anger can show up as agitation, disgust or resentment. Intense expressions of anger can be seen as fury, hostility and vengefulness.

Interestingly, just as people are afraid of anger and sadness, there is just as much aversion to 'positive' emotions, such as happiness. With happiness, people are concerned about appearing boastful and so downplay achievements or celebrations to prevent appearing proud or arrogant. Alternatively, people are concerned about appearing happy around those who may be doing it tough, and so hold back their joy out of respect for other people's feelings. As we will see, there are so many other important messages that our emotions are sending us. When we listen carefully, we can unravel the wisdom of our emotions.

Emotions Express Through the Body

One of the key reasons we are afraid of emotions is because of the uncomfortable feelings that they stir up in the body. We know from experience that when we get angry, we often clench our jaw and tense our shoulders. When we feel afraid, we often get queasy sensations in the stomach. When we get sad, our throat tightens and our eyes begin to water. But I think you would be amazed to see just how impactful emotions express themselves in the body. The following heat maps show where and how the body is affected by the emotions that arise[36].

This diagram provides so many insights. For example, for most emotions, the physical response is limited to one part of the body. Still, when we see happiness or love, we see a great spread of reaction throughout the body. These emotions touch every part of us, and why it certainly makes sense that they sit higher on the Levels of Consciousness. Our whole body becomes engaged with these higher-order emotions. Sadness shows the heat at the heart, throat and eyes, but interestingly the limbs become colder. As we have seen, shame shows up as a blend of sadness with cold limbs and fear with its signature red chest. The picture of depression is bleak indeed, with all limbs cold and a void at the heart. Depression then appears to be an absence of emotion at the heart centre. But just as we have seen with all emotions, even depression is not a permanent fixture and certainly does not define who we are.

'You don't have to be positive all the time. It's perfectly okay to feel sad, angry, annoyed, frustrated, scared and anxious. Having feelings doesn't make you a negative person. It makes you human.'

~ Lori Deschene

The message here is that your body is an amazing tool to help you understand what is going on for you emotionally. If you can bring awareness to your body and identify where you may be feeling heat, tightness, tingling or cold, then you have your first great clue as to what emotion is working its way through you.

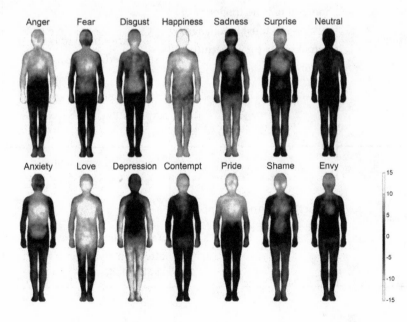

Figure 32 – Where Emotions Show Up In the Body

Emotions Send Important Messages

The emotions you are feeling hold a great deal of wisdom about what is happening for you at the moment. Emotions are actually calling us to grow in some way, but what way? What are emotions telling us? Here are some initial thoughts about the messages that emotions are giving us:

Emotion	Message	Action to grow
Anger	Something is no longer of service and must be changed to make way for something better.	Elimination of the old belief, behaviour or relationship to make way for new and better ways. Boundaries need to be established or enforced. Without giving an explanation, learn to just say 'no'.
Fear	Something important needs to be faced or learned	Become fully present and aware of what is going on for you. You will need to pay full attention and learn a new skill or behaviour.

Sadness	Something needs to be let go of. Something meaningful is going away. You need to stop denying reality.	Let go of a role, dream, behaviour or relationship that is no longer helpful for you to grow and bloom.
Happiness	Something or someone needs to be celebrated or appreciated.	Take time to celebrate yourself, others or something that you have witnessed. Allow yourself to experience full internal wellbeing.

Emotions are there for us to learn from, but first, we need to be aware of them and understand the messages that they are sending. For example, the sadness that Alice felt was a message that she needed to let go of her expectations of perfection. She needed to stop clinging to the idea that she will be judged by how she looks in her swimsuit. She needed to let go of the harsh self-judgment that she was ugly. She had to let go of the role of the sad girl sitting on the sand. By listening to her emotions and releasing behaviours that were not serving her, she was free to embrace and celebrate the whole amazing person she is, and create space to feel joy.

How Do You Deal with Emotions?

It is likely that throughout the course of your life, you have built automatic habits around emotions. Like thoughts, when difficult emotions arise, you may do things to avoid or repress them. You may distract yourself, numb out, over analyse the emotion or justify it in some way. Again, if you are experiencing really traumatic or distressing emotions, then distraction can be a valid short-term strategy. It can help you through the tsunami until you can feel the wave pass. But in the long term, ignoring feelings and the messages they send can be detrimental to your growth. The problem is, denying or repressing one emotion (because you consider it hurtful or negative) also turns off all the other emotions, including joy. Remember the Levels of Consciousness? To reach the emotions of love and joy, you need courage and acceptance, and that is for all of the experiences we have in our life.

So, take some time now to think about how you tend to react to the core emotions. What is your current pattern of behaviour when these emotions arise?:

Emotion	My usual behaviour
Anger	
Fear	
Sadness	
Happiness	

Caring for Difficult Emotions

Some emotions we feel can be very distressing and overwhelming. So what do we do when a large and painful wave comes our way? The process of caring for emotions is initially the same as caring for our thoughts.

1. Notice—as for thoughts, the first step in caring for difficult emotions is to be aware of what is happening. In the case of emotions, though, the best place to begin is by bringing awareness to what is occurring in your body. What do you feel is going on in your chest, throat, back, shoulders, eyes, belly and limbs? Pay attention to how the emotion is expressing itself in your body.

2. Name—give your feeling a name using one or more of the four core emotions: anger, sadness, fear or happiness. Say the following in your own mind, out loud or write it down:

    'I am feeling...'

    This allows you to keep the feeling in perspective and creates some distance to prevent you from getting stuck in a cognitive loop.

    The next two steps are somewhat different for emotions. They are:

3. Soothe the emotion—do the three-part deep breathing exercise we covered in Chapter 15. This will power up your stress-reduction mechanisms and help calm and soothe the emotion.

4. Wonder—when you sense that the wave is beginning to pass, the next step is to get curious. Look at the messages that the emotions are

sending you, how they are calling you to grow and ask yourself the following question:

'What is this emotion telling me?'

Facing your emotions like this, and opening up to the messages they are sending you, is one of the greatest acts of bravery. But like any new skill, it takes practise. Be gentle with yourself as you begin to care for your feelings. Show yourself great compassion and celebrate the courage you are taking to step into your unique beauty and way of being. Remember, while sometimes it does not feel like it, emotions are there as your friend, not your enemy. They will pass through and leave you with pearls of wisdom along the way, if you let them.

Now It's Your Turn

Think of an experience you have had lately with one of the four core emotions. See if you can choose one that was intense and is still clear in your mind. Replay the experience in your mind and ask yourself the following questions:

- What were the one or more four core emotions I was feeling?

- How did this emotion express itself in my body?

- What was my reaction to this emotion?

- What did I end up doing as a result of this feeling?

- Thinking back on the situation now, what do I think the emotion was trying to tell me?

- How was this emotion helping me to grow?

WHAT NEXT?

If there is one thing that can sidetrack or stall your expedition to blooming, it is the discomfort of troubling emotions. As you have seen, emotions can cause short-term disruptions in our physical state (such as muscle tension, nausea and increased heart rate), but if denied or repressed can also cause long-term suffering. Therefore it is so natural that we would try to avoid emotions. But it is only through having the courage to work through the full range of our emotions that we can reach a point of self-appreciation. Then only by having even more courage to move forward can we find a place of joy and peace for ourselves. We cannot pick and choose the experiences we have in this life, we can only choose how we react to them.

Remembering, emotions deliver important messages about how we are travelling on our expedition and any actions that we need to take to keep us moving towards our daily blooming. Now that you have learned to care for your emotions, you can step forward with greater confidence to make peace with your body, which is ultimately peace with yourself. But first, there is one more area of yourself that we must acknowledge, respect and care for, and that is your spirituality. Here I don't mean religion; I mean our sense of meaning and purpose in this world. It is our 'why' our reason for embarking on this expedition in the first place. In the next chapter, we will consider how you define and achieve your meaningful difference in this world and fulfil your unique and amazing potential.

'Your intellect may be confused, but your emotions will never lie to you.'
~ Roger Ebert

COMMITMENT STATEMENT

I commit to caring for my emotions, both positive
and negative, as an ally on my expedition to bloom.
I commit to letting them pass through and working
with the messages that they send to allow
myself to fully bloom.

CHAPTER EIGHTEEN

Caring for Your Spirit

'Nothing is more powerful than the human spirit.'
~ Charlie Grant

What is the Spirit?

Every part of this book so far has been leading you to here, the inevitable important chapter. For now, it is where we begin to take the acceptance, compassion and care you show your body, mind and emotions, and use this to move forward in ways that are meaningful for you. Now comes the real expedition of sharing your unique self with the world. Throughout this book, I have said that one key role of your body is as a home to your unique spirit, the seed within. But what does that mean? What is the spirit?

Depending on your background, the word 'spirit' can have a variety of different connotations. Some may think of Christian religious references to the Holy Spirit. Others may liken it to the concept of soul or Atman in Hinduism. Others may conceptualise ghosts or ethereal manifestations. The way I use the notion of spirit in this book is to refer to those qualities that are unique to you and only experienced by you, and which go beyond your body, mind and emotions.

Spirit is the part of us that cannot be found—it has no physical location—and yet it is our very essence. Spirit is the call within us to reach beyond where we are now, to surpass materialistic boundaries and to live aligned with our highest values. It is comprised of those values we hold dear and our vision of how we can bloom in this world. Spirit touches every part of our being. Here are some other words that may be more familiar to you to describe what spirit is:

- A sense of purpose

- Meaning in life

- Faith

- Wholeness

- Power within

- Oneness

- Innermost self

- Connectedness

- Vibe

Connection with Our Spirit

Perhaps spirit is more easily understood when we can see what it looks like. Wayne Dyer describes what it looks like to be connected to your spirit:

'Strong emotions such as passion and bliss are indications that you're connected to spirit, or "inspired", if you will. When you're inspired, you activate dormant forces, and the abundance you seek in any form comes streaming into your life.'

~ Wayne Dyer

This quote suggests that being connected to your spirit looks like operating at the higher levels of consciousness. Love, joy and peace are present, and you are experiencing synchronicity and extraordinary outcomes. Connection with spirit means loving what makes you unique and being immune from the dramas, negativity or opinions of anyone or anything outside of yourself. You have a solid anchor that keeps you grounded as the winds and storms of life swirl around you. However, more than that, you have a clear sense of purpose for this life; a North Star that guides your daily travels.

But what does it look like to be disconnected from your spirit? You can imagine the opposite. Losing connection with your spirit is like operating from the lower levels of consciousness. It is full of pride, anger, fear, apathy, guilt and shame. It is constantly being battered around by external events, and the actions and opinions of others. You know you have lost touch with your spirit if you spend your days feeling anguish, hurt, shame or frustration.

Being connected with our spirits sounds so wonderful. So, the next question is why do we allow ourselves to get disconnected from our spirit? The reality is that disconnection from spirit is largely an unconscious process. The world we live in is a very busy one. We are constantly exposed to news and social media, which draw us into the lives of others. Every time we see and react to a situation outside of ourselves, then we are beginning the process of disconnection.

Imagine spending the day on YouTube, Facebook and Instagram. After a whole day engaged in other people's lives, it is highly likely that you would feel separated from yourself. If you have children or are living with other family members or friends, then you are constantly exposed to other people's happiness, successes, dilemmas and despair. If we are not conscious and careful, all of these distractions around us create the risk of self-disconnection. Before you know it, you wake up one morning and wonder: *What is my purpose in life?* I know I did.

What is Spirituality?

The reality is that we all go through cycles of connection and disconnection with our spirit. The difference between people is how long these cycles of disconnection last. For some people who have braved the wilds of self-awareness and compassion, they may 'lose themselves' for a few hours but then realise they are lost and take action to connect again. They may recalibrate quickly, find their North Star again and continue the journey.

For others who have not yet embarked on a journey of self-discovery, they could spend most of this lifetime disconnected from their unique and beautiful seed. They are not really sure what they are here for and have never been compelled to look for their North Star. They muddle around repeating the same daily patterns and staying in their current zones of safety. It is likely that they are doing all the things that society tells them will create success, but are still frustrated and dissatisfied with life.

This is where spirituality comes in. Spirituality is not something you have, but is taking proactive action to maintain the connection with your spirit. Just like we eat well to keep our bodies healthy, spiritual practices help us stay in close contact with our spirit—our most powerful force.

Being spiritual, then, means to be living authentically. You are aware:

- That you are on your own unique journey;
- Of what you offer to others;

- That the way you bloom will be unique to you as it is also unique to others;

- That you have an ongoing relationship with your inner wisdom; and

- That worries, conflict and fear will still be present, but with your connection to spirit, they have no power to control you or stop you blooming. You understand that all emotions are simply messages to listen to.

- You stem from love for all.

Examples of Spiritual Practice

Spiritual practice is just like our daily regimens. It is something that we dedicate ourselves to doing to help us stay in connection with our seed and live in a way that we can be true to its purpose. Spiritual practice allows us to be more accepting and compassionate towards ourselves and others. It helps us see the bigger picture of our lives and what we contribute to the world.

When you think of spiritual practice, though, you may immediately conjure thoughts of attending religious services, chanting or praying. Yes, these are certainly some examples of spiritual practice. But just as each person is unique, so is the type of practice that helps align you to your spirit. It can be any kind of activity that calls you to not only look inwards, but to make a contribution to something bigger than ourselves. For example, spiritual practices can include:

- Spending time in nature—being still, appreciating and caring for the natural wonders around you.

- Organised religion—attending religious ceremonies or prayers provide an important sense of community and purpose.

- Meditation—sitting in stillness to connect with your spirit.

- Prayer or contemplation—becoming attuned with our struggles and aligned with the power within us and around us.

- Creative pursuits—all forms of art, music and dance help us connect to the passion within and allow us to express it in the world.

Identifying the spiritual practices that are meaningful for you is a vital step on your path to blooming. Because the further you go on this expedition, the more you will need to rely on your North Star to guide and motivate you to continue. Leading a naturally blooming life does not mean you will be without worries. In fact, it is likely you will encounter more conflict as you finally have the strength to use your voice and live by your values.

The Journey of the Spirit

If you remember in the discussion of the Levels of Consciousness in Chapter 3, you learned that the lower levels of consciousness are not lesser or worse than those at the higher levels. In fact, the lower levels of consciousness are the gates to our learning and growth. We must pass through shame, guilt, fear, apathy, anger and pride before we can progress to acceptance, love and joy. While we might prefer to just jump to joy, the reality is that we have to work through these 'uncomfortable' states to become our true selves. These lower states are the fuel that gets us to the higher levels of consciousness.

So just as I have shown you, people's attitudes towards beauty are simply a matter of maturity, and the extent to which you are living true to your seed is also. When you are in the early stages of self-development, enacting your spirit may take a back seat to acceptance from others and conformity with society. These all exert forces upon you that influence your behaviour. However, with the courage to question, to understand and be true to yourself, you can begin to choose actions that are life-promoting, encouraging and supportive to expressing your true self into the world. With courage, you can tap into your own power to thrive.

The message here is that it does not matter where you are right now on your journey. The most exciting thing is that you are on The Expedition and moving closer to blooming. Start where you are, with what you have, and continue the journey to self-discovery and reconnection with your true self. Keep looking forwards knowing where you have come from, and where you are going towards the bright and beautiful vision of you in full bloom.

How Do You Care for Your Spirit?

Now, there are three things that you can do to help you get in touch with and stay connected with your seed. These are:

1.   Getting clear on your values;

2.   Living by your values; and

3.   Dedicating time to spiritual practice.

Getting Clear on Your Values

Values are the ultimate benchmark of your life. They indicate what direction you want to take in *your* life, and what you believe is important. Notice the emphasis on the word 'your' here. If you are living by the values of others, for fear of not fitting in, then you put yourself at risk for all of the symptoms of disconnection with spirit. You are sacrificing what is truly meaningful and important to you for the relative comfort of conformity. But here is the kicker:

'You can choose courage, or you can choose comfort,
but you can't choose both.'
~ Brené Brown

Living by the values of others is not going to allow you to live authentically and to be true to your spirit. It is a sure way to end up years from now feeling very dissatisfied. You need to have the courage to dig deep and identify those values that are yours, and then take the next step to live by them each day.

I completely understand that if you have been living in the shadow of others for so long, you may feel that you really don't know what your values are anymore. Honestly, I don't think many of us stop to consider them at all. Usually, we only question our values during times of crisis or intense conflict.

So, here is my gift to you. Today, you have the chance to spend some time figuring out what is really important for you. How do you want to live *your* life? To do this, head to Appendix 3, which provides a starting list of values for you. Note that this list is not comprehensive, and you may develop some others that aren't on the list , the importance here is choosing ones that resonate best for you. Tick those that do resonate for you—that really feel 'right' for you— and write down any others that come to mind. This exercise is not for anyone else. It is all about you!

Then write down what you feel would be your top six values. In the next section, we will work through what living these values at their best looks like for you. So, for now, just develop your list of the values that are most meaningful for you.

Living by Your Values

Values really are meaningless unless they are being enacted. That is, the only time a value can actually exist is when it is captured in your behaviour. When we choose an action that supports our value, the value is alive at that moment. For example, if you value 'authenticity', then this value only exists when you choose actions that are in line with being authentic, such as honouring your whole self and allowing yourself to express and be seen in the world. Until then, it is really only a wish or idea.

It is normal for us, though, to not always follow our values. For example, in some instances where we have obstacles that we must face, it might be challenging for us to live in line with our values. Other people make demands of us, and we feel compelled to help others solve their problems and ease their distress. We get sucked into the cries of our self-esteem and take actions to secure our place, some of which we later feel remorse for. This happens to each and every one of us. Whenever we get trapped into fear, anger, guilt, shame or pride, we can behave in ways that are sometimes in direct opposition to our true intentions.

This is where self-compassion is so important. Rather than beating ourselves up and punishing ourselves for deviations from our values, self-compassion helps us acknowledge and care for the choice we felt we had to make in that moment and the suffering it has created. It helps us learn from our actions and the consequences. It helps us attune to our emotions and acknowledges the gut feeling that we have become misaligned to our true self. Self-compassion prepares us to act differently next time this opportunity arises.

'Tell me what you value, and I might believe you,
but show me your calendar and your bank statement,
and I'll show you what you really value.'
~ Peter Drucker

While this may be a simplistic view of the world, it is not too left field. Where we put all of our resources, time, energy and money reveals what is important to us. Take a moment to do a quick stocktake of how you are currently living your values. Give yourself a star rating for the amount of investment you are making into your top six values.

Value	How well am I currently living this value because of how much investment this value receives in terms of my time, energy and money?
	★ ★ ★ ★ ★
	★ ★ ★ ★ ★
	★ ★ ★ ★ ★
	★ ★ ★ ★ ★
	★ ★ ★ ★ ★

For those values that you rated low on your current investment, are there areas in which you can put more attention to enact these more in your life? For example, if self-respect is one of your key values, then how can you enact this more in your leisure time or relationships? Could you decide not to spend time with those around you that bring you down and insult you? Maybe you could decide not to excessively drink and instead use this time and energy for investment in another value, such as health, by going for a nature hike or sunset walk with a friend?

To live the values you have listed that are important to you, will you need some assistance by making changes in your:

- Work or career choices

- Relaxation and sleep habits

- Eating habits

- Exercise regimen

- Relationship and support networks

- Recreation and leisure activities

- Spiritual practices

Ultimately, the process of blooming is founded on your freely chosen values. These values support the way you really want to live your life and will motivate you every day to pursue your dreams and life direction. They are not commitments you make to yourself every time you read a self-help book. Values help you make the best decisions each day and every moment. These choices can bring you closer to your spirit or take you further away. The choice really is yours and your values are yours to choose and change as you need.

Dedicating Time for Spiritual Practice

Spiritual practice is essential for us to foster our seed and to allow us to bloom into our unique beauty. However, it has been so misunderstood and has not been given the due attention and respect it deserves. Remember Wayne Dyer's quote: 'Strong emotions such as passion and bliss are indications that you're connected to spirit.'

So spiritual practice does come down to taking the time to do what you love—those things that create passion and joy in your life. The only problem is that many of these activities can be judged by others as laziness, silliness or just a waste of time. When you say you are going to meditate, paint, dance, hike in the forest or play sport, there can be a real sense that others may think you are being selfish. After all, isn't there some help that is needed around the house? Shouldn't you be cleaning, studying, working or doing something more productive? What people miss with this perspective is that spiritual practice is essential to restore our energy for the tasks ahead. We need to have energy to make values-based choices moment by moment. Taking time to undertake spiritual practice is an investment in our own wellbeing that, in fact, then radiates out to help others.

The Dalai Lama suggests that there are actually two forms of selfishness. One is called 'foolish selfishness' and the other is 'wise selfishness'. Here is how he distinguishes between the two:

'It is important that when pursuing our own self-interest,
we should be "wise selfish" and not "foolish selfish".
Being foolish selfish means pursuing our own interests in a narrow,
short-sighted way. Being wise selfish means taking a broader view and
recognising that our own long-term individual interest lies in the welfare
of everyone. Being wise selfish means being compassionate.'
~ Dalai Lama

So if taking the time out for that art class, that run or to watch the clouds pass by helps open our mind and heart, to help us connect with our seed, then it is wise selfishness. In fact, if we don't do these things, the result is usually that we start getting grumpy, pessimistic and not nice to be around at all. It appears then that by not taking time for spiritual practice, we are actually exhibiting foolish selfishness. By denying ourselves the things that bring us peace and happiness, our ability to bloom is affected and our interactions with others are compromised too.

Caring for your spirit is one of the bravest and most compassionate things you can do. By taking the time to connect with and nurture what makes you unique, you are leaving a personal legacy in this world. You are also sending ripples of empowerment and confidence out to all the women, girls and people around you.

WHAT NEXT?

Your spirit, that I lovingly call your seed (interchangeably), is the combination of qualities, values, passions and dreams that make you the unique person that you are. While it has no physical location, your body is its home. Your body, mind and emotions provide care for and connection with your seed. What you do with your body, mind and emotions can either bring you in alignment with your seed or move you further away from it.

As you undertake your expedition to blooming, your spirit will become your North Star. Your values will help you make choices in every moment, and those choices will determine how you show up in this world. Do you show up connected and aligned with your spirit? Do you move forward consciously and with confidence and compassion? Or do you show up disconnected and isolated from your true power, drowning in fear, anger and pride?

In the next chapter, things get very exciting. All the work you have done to date is going to be brought together to paint the picture of what it looks like for you to bloom—physically, mentally, emotionally and spiritually. You are now the creator of your life and understand all of the elements you need to live confidently and to bloom. It is now time to begin the greatest masterpiece that has ever been made: the true and beautiful you!

COMMITMENT STATEMENT

I commit to connecting with and caring for my unique and beautiful spirit. I commit to standing by the values that are true to me and doing all I can to let my spirit shine.

CHAPTER NINETEEN

What Does Blooming Look Like for You?

'Beauty held is the seed. Beauty shared is the flower.'

~ Adapted from John Harrigan

Visualise Your Blooming

If the last chapter on caring for your spirit was one of the most important concepts of this book, then this chapter is the most exciting. In this chapter, you get to use the wonderful gift that is your imagination to conjure the vision of what it looks like for you to bloom. We are going to use the power of visualisation to set you on the courageous path to being at peace with your body and allowing yourself to bloom in the world.

While visualisation may sound like a bit of fun, which it certainly is, it is also an essential step to make your future a reality. We have seen how our bodies, thoughts, emotions and spirit are linked, with each having the ability to lift the other up or to bring each other down. Visualisation starts with our thoughts and uses their power to positively influence the body, emotions and spirit. The thing is, you can have all the best intentions in the world to move forward with courage and consciousness. But like anything new, unless we know where we are going, we don't know what action to take. Then when we have decided on the best action to take, it is about continuing to repeat it until it becomes natural and second nature for us to do.

The Science Behind Visualisation

Visualisation is also called mental practice or guided imagery. It has been found to not only improve psychological skills, but physical skills as well. Still, even more importantly, you can do it from the comfort of the sanctuary you created in Chapter 13!

This was certainly the case for Emily Cook, who is an Olympic freestyle skier. Emily suffered a series of injuries and was unable to train for two years. She was told it was just too hard to return to competing after this long time away. Still, she used visualisation as the key ally in her recovery process. Emily recorded her visualisations so that she could play them repeatedly throughout the day. Here is a short sample of what she included in her visualisations[37]:

'I would say into the recorder: "I'm standing on the top of
the hill. I can feel the wind on the back of my neck. I can hear
the crowd…" going through all those different senses and then

actually going through what I wanted to do for the perfect jump. "I turn down the in-run. I stand up. I engage my core. I look at the top of the jump." I was going through every little step of how I wanted that jump to turn out. I don't think I could possibly do a jump, or especially a new trick, without having this imagery process... For me, this is so very key to the athlete I have become.'

Researchers have found that the same neural patterns occur when a person imagines something happening as when the real event is happening[38]. So for Emily, simply visualising a jump begins a cascade of reactions in the brain, including the activation of attention, planning, motor control and memory. These are the same processes that occur during the real activity. Your brain is stimulated the same way whether you're physically performing an action or simply visualising it happening.

What Does This Mean for You?

This scientific evidence means that you have an incredible ally on your journey to blooming. One of the key parts of the brain stimulated through visualisation is the reticular activating system (RAS). This is the neurological system that acts as your lookout system, constantly scanning the environment, finding opportunities for you to achieve a goal. For example, when this system receives messages that your body needs food, it begins scanning the environment for possible sources of nutrition. It is the RAS that is going to work as you explore the pantry shelves for a snack or meal.

When the goal is something more important, such as sharing your unique seed with the world, this system lights up again and begins looking for ways that you can make it happen. When you imagine your goal, the brain really does not distinguish between this being your vision and this being reality. The result is that the RAS fires up regardless to help you find options and solutions to achieve your goal.

Visualisation helps you practise behaviours that will help you bloom from the safety of your own home. The ability to repeat actions that are new or challenging frequently will enable confidence to be gained much faster. Visualising what blooming looks like for you provides real hope that it is possible, and provides a sense of control over your own behaviours and thus the outcomes you are wanting to achieve.

That is why I recommend visualisation becomes a key part of your *Body Beautiful* journey. You need to see what blooming looks like for you to create the impetus and motivation to begin making the shifts that will help you fully appreciate and be your true self. Then you need the confidence to continue when obstacles or adversity arise along the way. Both initial motivation and sustained effort are key outcomes of the visualisation process. So, by now, I am sure you are so keen to get started. Let me walk you through the steps to help you bloom.

The Keys to Visualisation

To get your mind working in your favour and to harness the power of visualisation, there is a specific approach to use. It is a method that was developed by Soviet sports trainers in the 1970s. Since then, people have used it across the world to make their dreams a reality. The key is to engage all of your senses when practising to create a rich and full mental experience. The more sensory stimuli you can include in the visualisation, the more realistic it will seem to the mind and therefore the more effective your visualisation will be. The main senses called on during mental practice include:

- Visual—such as pictures and images in the mind;

- Auditory—such as people speaking or music; and

- Kinaesthetic—involving how the body feels and physical reactions.

However, several people also enjoy incorporating smells and tastes into their practice. These sensory experiences are then combined with emotions, to create an incredible potential for change.

So, now is your chance to use the tool of mental practice to achieve what is important to you. Are you ready to begin the great adventure into your blooming? Let's go!

What it Looks Like to Bloom

Step 1 – Prepare Your Body

It is important that during the visualisation practice you are relaxed, able to breathe calmly and focused. Your time is precious, and you want to make sure you are using it wisely. For this reason, preparing your physical foundation is the essential first step. Two options include:

1. Seated. Sit on the edge of a chair with your feet flat on the floor. This will prevent you from slumping back into the chair and restricting your breath.

2. Laying down. Lay on the ground and use a block or cushion under your knees to take the pressure off your lower back and to keep your spine supported.

Step 2 – Define the Goal

Visualisation is all about creating a mental image of an outcome that you are seeking. In this case, your goal is to have your unique beauty bloom in this world.

You could, of course, come up with a more specific goal such as:

- Becoming more confident or in control in a specific area of life. For example, socialising or self-care;

- Living aligned with one of your core values, such as self-respect or creativity; or

- Doing something that you have always dreamed of doing. For example, wearing a bikini for the first time ever.

Still, if nothing springs to mind, the following questions may be of assistance to help you develop your goal:

- Who do you want to be?

- What do you want to do?

- How do you want to feel?

Step 3 – Imagine Achieving the Goal

Now you have defined the goal you will be visualising, it is time to get sensory! Make sure you are comfortable, and then imagine yourself succeeding in that goal. Take your time here—give yourself space to create the vision of your blooming. Don't worry if nothing visual appears in your mind, as visualisation is a skill that does take practise. The following action of bringing your other senses into play should help.

As you read previously, the more sensory stimuli you can bring into your visualisation, the more effective the process is. Here are some questions you can work through to engage your senses in painting a full and rich experience of your success:

- Where are you?

- What does your physical environment look like?

- What noises are coming from your surroundings?

- What is the temperature like?

- What are you wearing?

- Who is around you, and what are they doing?

- What are the people around you saying?

- Are there any specific smells or tastes that you can sense around you?

- How are you feeling?

- What emotions are arising within you as you are blooming in this world?

If you are still stuck, I love to use the exercise with my clients with the question "But if I did know, what blooming would look like for me, what comes to mind?" Noting that no idea or thought is wrong or silly, just notice everything that comes to mind. Remembering, your seed always knows so trust what is coming to you. You can always see soon, if it feels right for your visualisation now in the next step.

Step 4 – Write it Down

While visualisation provides a boost to your success, writing down your goals and plans adds another layer of support. It has been shown that people who write down their goals are significantly more likely to achieve them.[39] To assist, here is a table of all of the topics we have covered in the book so far. You have made it so far in this journey already. Now, to continue moving forward, start getting specific about how your life looks when you are blooming in this world.

Area of my life	What blooming looks like for me
My beliefs—what are the fundamental beliefs I am living by?	
My values—what values are guiding my actions every day?	
Where am I living?	
What are my living surroundings like?	
What does my social network look like?	
Who is on my Body Beautiful team? (coaches, doctors, teammates, fans).	
How am I caring for my body?	
What am I eating and drinking?	
What is my sleep pattern like?	
How am I exercising?	
What am I doing to care for negative thoughts?	
What am I doing to care for uncomfortable emotions?	
What am I doing to live by my values?	

You can use the information you have written down to prepare and record a script for your visualisation. Just like Emily did, you can then listen to it every day as a guided imagery activity to catapult you forward to your full and beautiful blooming.

Step 5 – And Repeat... Daily

'Practise is the hardest part of learning, and training is the essence of transformation.'
~ Ann Voskamp

While I wish I could tell you that just one visualisation session will bring instantaneous blooming, it is so very far from the truth. We have seen in the Confidence Cycle in Chapter 11 that it is only practise—continued repetition—that creates the new beliefs, behaviours and habits that will help you to bloom. New neural pathways take time to build, but they are guaranteed to build quicker the more regularly you practise. It is better to do five minutes of visualisation every day rather than a half an hour a week. Why is this? It is due to the remarkable gift called the 'compound effect'.

Let me show you how it works. Say you are living your normal day, every day of the year. The maths equation for this is $1^{365} = 1$. If you just keep continuing as normal, nothing will change. Now, what if you add just an extra 1 per cent onto your day? That is, we make your day 1.01 instead of 1. Look at the remarkable increase that happens: $1.01^{365} = 37.8$.

By adding just one extra per cent, you have improved your outcome by almost thirty-eight times what you were achieving just living out your normal days. By doing this 1 extra per cent every single day over the year, you can make incredible growth.

Of course, if you only do the 1 per cent once a month, you will get some improvement in outcomes: $1.01^{12} = 1.13$. If you do the visualisation once a week, there is a slightly better result: $1.01^{52} = 1.7$. But this is still far from the thirty-eight times benefit you will achieve from doing the visualisation every day. Goals are achieved and visions become a reality when you take small actions consistently every day. These actions do only need to be very small. If you equate your self-development—your journey to blooming—as a full-time job, then 1 per cent of eight hours a day (the standard full-time work hours) is just under five minutes! Can you create five minutes in your day to work towards your blooming? If you do, you can be guaranteed that this time next year you will be in a position thirty-eight times better than where you are now.

I suspect that if you do commit to doing this visualisation each day, you will be living a very different life by this time next year. This is because of another very important principle called the 'ripple effect'. This tells us that when we make changes in one area of our life, this sends ripples out to every other area. These areas of life are shown in the Wheel of Life[40].

Figure 33 – The Wheel of Life

Let's work through Alice's example. She put aside her fears about being seen in a swimsuit and spent the afternoon swimming in the ocean. This one act of living her core values creates the following ripples:

- The physical stimulation from the sun, the sea and the exercise makes her feel really happy (mental and educational);

- Her positive mental state encourages her to choose supportive lunch options (physical and health);

- Enjoying time with her friends has established stronger relationship bonds (social and cultural);

- She is in a better mood and therefore less reactive to family taunts and teasing and more supportive of family members (family and home); and

- She is inspired by the ocean and decides to take up painting lessons so that she can relive the experience regularly (spiritual and ethical).

That one act has created so many positive effects in Alice's life. This can happen for you too if you take just five minutes each day to visualise your blooming in this world.

So beautiful, where will you schedule your five minutes?

WHAT NEXT?

Repetition is the only way to build new neural pathways that will support your *Body Beautiful* behaviours and habits. But we may not often get the chance to practise regularly enough. So, to speed up the process, we can use visualisation as part of our practice regimen. The potential benefits of visualisation because of guided imagery are astounding. Still, there is no getting around the work that must be done to reap the benefits in your life and for your confidence. Remembering, this work can be done from the comfort of your own sanctuary. So, get comfortable and visualise your blooming into reality.

Simply put, if you are committed to sharing your unique and incredible spirit with the world, then visualisation is an activity that will speed up your journey. Visualisation is a very smart and effective tool to help get you where you want to go as efficiently and effectively as possible.

However, I really do understand that there are many obstacles ahead of you on this journey. Other people construct many of these, and many come from our own limiting beliefs and behaviours. It is scary to reach out into the unknown, and fear is a powerful repressive force. Nevertheless, there is nothing that cannot be overcome with planning and perseverance. In the next chapter, we will cover the kind of obstacles you may encounter on your journey to blooming and help you plan in advance for how to move through them with care and compassion.

COMMITMENT STATEMENT

I commit to envisioning my blooming with great
belief and excitement. I commit to giving
myself the best chance to achieve my goals by taking
time each day to mentally practise visualising
my full blooming.

CHAPTER TWENTY
Caring for Obstacles and Crises

'You may encounter many defeats, but you must not be defeated.
It may be necessary to encounter the defeats, so you can know who you are,
what you can rise from, how you can still come out of it.'

~ Maya Angelou

Obstacles Are Inevitable

As much as I am wishing you a journey full of sunny days, soft breezes and easy roads, I know that this will not be your reality. In fact, I would be doing you a great disservice by not helping you understand that the obstacles you face on your journey are both:

- Inevitable; and

- The greatest gifts you will encounter.

Difficulties and challenges on your way to blooming are inevitable for one single reason: you are doing things that are completely new to you. In order to grow and to bloom, you need to change, which means there will be behaviours, actions, people and situations you have never encountered before or that you are truly seeing them for what they are. It is inevitable that you will need to strengthen your self-confidence muscle. Knowing the first few times there may be blunders, mistakes and lessons, but as we have seen in the Confidence Cycle, this is all part of the process of learning new skills. When you first learned to walk, you stumbled and fell. When you first learned to ride a bike, you wobbled and tipped over. When you first learned to read, words and letters got jumbled. Also, of course, who can forget the adventure of learning to drive? I am still amazed that my parents' car made it out of that experience alive. All the adults around you knew that these struggles were part of the learning process. It was just your turn to be the learner who had to go through it.

Your journey to blooming is no different. I've made it clear that the lower levels of consciousness are the fuel for our growth and maturity. There are days you will get stuck in the mud of guilt or fear, or be fired by the flames of anger or pride. These states of consciousness don't just disappear because you want them to. The growth occurs by learning how to work through them with awareness and acceptance. You reach your goals by facing them with courage and compassion.

Obstacles Are the Greatest Gift

While it may not feel like it at the time, every time you encounter an obstacle on your path, you have received the greatest gift. How else are you going to grow if you don't get the chance to practise the skills of blooming? Every obstacle then is a wonderful chance to practise, and another step along the path of your blooming potential and growth. If you see challenges on the path as burdens, then they become a force upon you and you are immediately drawn into the lower levels of consciousness. However, if you can see them as a chance to nurture and build your own curiosity with confidence, and treat them with acceptance and love, then you will receive the greatest gift into your own understanding.

At the end of the day, you cannot control what happens to you. But you can control how you react to what happens. It is up to you whether you choose to react in a way that is going to keep you stuck in behaviours and emotions that limit your growth. Or whether you choose to react in a way that will help you bloom. I remember hearing a story of a Buddhist monk who had an incredibly annoying assistant. All of the students begged the monk to get rid of the assistant, saying he was impossible to work with. The monk, however, stated that this was the exact reason he kept him close. You see, the monk realised that he was not going to be able to develop his qualities of patience and compassion without practise. This assistant was giving him lots of practise! This seems odd in our world, doesn't it? It is more common for us to try and remove difficulties altogether.

The reality is that every challenge is a gift to you, but it is up to you whether you are ready to accept it at the time. There is no doubt that some days you will be able to take that gift, learn and grow. Other days may feel all too hard, and you will walk away from the gift. In the end, though, either choice is empowering if it is done with consciousness and care for yourself. Either choice is perfect if it is done from a place of life-affirming power and not external life-crushing force.

The Two Types of Obstacles

The types of obstacles you will encounter on your journey will be either:

1. External obstacles—people or events that occur outside of your control; or
2. Internal obstacles—beliefs, thoughts, feelings or behaviours that are within your control.

External obstacles include:

*   Stress applied by other people;
*   Criticism by other people;
*   Lack of support provided by others; or
*   Events occurring in:
    *   ◊ Politics
    *   ◊ The environment
    *   ◊ Social trends
    *   ◊ Health, including pandemics
    *   ◊ Technological advancements

◊   Laws and regulations

◊   The economy

Internal obstacles include:

- Unhelpful thoughts and painful memories;

- Justifying your unhelpful behaviours;

- Procrastinating;

- Judgements about yourself;

- Distressing emotions;

- Fear of others' opinions, change or failure;

- Inability to see other people's options; or

- Limited resources—for example, time, money or energy.

For example, say you have taken up a regular yoga practice and find the physical and spiritual benefits life-changing for you. The studio is right next to your work, so it is very convenient. You go to yoga early, shower and head to work feeling refreshed and positive for the day. Life is wonderful! But then, the yoga studio closes down. The lack of a yoga studio close to work is an external obstacle on your path to blooming. However, if you are unable to see other options to achieve this goal, then you are facing an internal obstacle as well. You could become angry, bitter and sad. This may even cause you to cease your practice. Or, if you are ready to see this as a gift, then you may be able to ask what opportunity this external event is providing. Perhaps it is calling you to:

- Seek out other studios where you can try a different style of yoga.

After all, you have been very curious to see what hot yoga would be like!

- Find a way to be more self-sufficient. This could be your opportunity to set up a studio in your own home. You have been thinking about how you could get more yoga into your life, and this could be the push you need to create your own daily practice.

Revisiting the Decision-Making Matrix

The Decision-Making Matrix we used in Chapter 16 is also invaluable to guide you through obstacles as they arise. When you encounter a challenge or difficulty, it is easy to get swept up in it and lose perspective about what the best action is to take in the situation. You can get drawn into rumination about external events and lose focus about what you actually have control over. You can waste so much time and energy worrying or trying to fix other people or things, when the most important thing at the time may be caring for yourself. Use the Decision-Making Matrix to help you allocate your time and energy wisely.

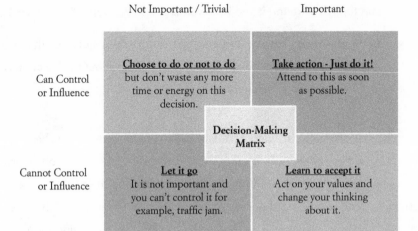

Figure 34 – The Decision-Making Matrix

You will see that there are two axes to this matrix. The first is the level of importance of this event to you. Note this importance is to you, not others. The second axis is the level of influence or control you have over the situation. Looking at these two elements then provides guidance as to what is the most appropriate action, with the four options being:

- Take action—where a situation is important to you, and you have control over it. Just take action as soon as possible.

- Choose to do or not to do—if you do have control over a situation. If it is not really that important, then the action is to make a decision quickly about what you are going to do and just stick to it. Don't waste further time or energy on worrying or thinking about it, as the outcome is not that important to you anyway.

- Accept it—this can be difficult. But if you have no power over a situation, even if it is vitally important to you, then it is futile to battle with it. There is nothing you can do but to work with your own beliefs and thoughts around it and keep yourself well throughout the process.

- Let it go—if you have neither care nor control for a situation, then let it go and move on. Spending any time ruminating about the situation is just a waste of your precious energy.

The first two options, where you have some control, present the challenge of taking action. Sometimes it takes great courage to take action on things that are important to us. So, in these situations, finding the motivation and strength to do something about it can be the greatest obstacle. For the latter two options, the challenge is to deal with unhelpful or distressing thoughts and emotions. When you can't control a situation, you feel helpless. You may see so much that is wrong occurring around you but feel helpless to change things. In this situation, the techniques for dealing with difficult thoughts and emotions covered in Chapters 16 and 17 are vital. Unhooking yourself from negative thoughts and caring for distressing emotions are your way through these events. These techniques will release you from the mental and emotional traps they create and allow you to use your time and energy on those things where you can make a difference.

Reactions From Others

The Decision-Making Matrix is a wonderful tool. However, it does simplify just how complex things can get when you are faced with criticism or unsupportive reactions from other people. You may notice, the further you grow and develop that some people around you already may become more critical, and here's why. You see, while you are committed to moving up the levels of consciousness, some people are very much stuck in the mire of grief, fear and guilt. They could be so blinded by these forces that they genuinely think your actions towards growth are dangerous or wrong. Or if they have desired the freedom you are seeking, they may be forced to reflect on their own lives and anger or pride may result from their own past failures and life frustrations. When you are faced with negative reactions from others, there are three simple rules you can apply:

1. Other peoples' opinions are about them and their life frustrations. Leave them with their own battles and do not engage in disagreements that are ultimately not about you at all.

2. Their actions indicate their level of maturity. I have said throughout this book that there is no right or wrong when it comes to behaviour and beliefs of beauty. It is simply a matter of maturity. These people are reacting from old and negative mindsets, and you know how difficult these are because you have been there yourself. Their reaction does not make them a bad person; it just shows their current level of maturity. Do not judge them for this, but practise compassion where you can.

3. It's your reaction that matters. Ultimately, how people treat you is up to them. You can't control what others do or say. You can only control your reaction. It is your choice whether you fall down and meet them in a place of anger, guilt or pride, or whether you can catch triggering thoughts and keep operating from a place of acceptance and love. As we have covered in Chapter 14, sometimes the best reaction is to distance ourselves from these people for both your and their own wellbeing.

'How people treat you is their karma;
how you react is yours.'
~ Wayne Dyer

Planning Ahead

You would not embark on a long road trip without making some plans in terms of directions, stopovers and how you will keep yourself sheltered and nourished along the way. Likewise, you would not plant a seed and then just leave it alone and hope for the best. To give it the best chance to grow and bloom, you would put together a watering and feeding regimen. You would think about the best location and shelter from weather and predators. The same holds true for your journey to blooming. It is both prudent and wise to put some thought into the obstacles you may face along the way and make plans in advance for how you will deal with them.

Take some time to identify and write down the types of obstacles you imagine may present themselves as you learn and grow. While there may be some external obstacles you can predict, such as criticism from others, the focus will mainly be on internal obstacles. Refer back to the examples presented at the beginning of the chapter and see which ones may be relevant for you.

It does not matter how many or how few obstacles you have on your list.

The most important thing is that you are already bringing awareness to those things that can create barriers to your blooming. Now it is time to put plans in place so that if these disruptions do arise, you are ready and they will not hold you back. For each obstacle on your list, prepare an 'if-then' plan. That is, 'if' the obstacle happens, 'then' I will take this action.

For example, it is highly likely that no matter how committed Alice is to going and having a great time at the beach with her friends, when the time comes closer it may begin to feel too hard. She may start to have worries and doubts. So, she can put together a backup plan that might go like this:

If I feel worried about going to the beach and think about not going, then I will:

- Phone a friend to provide support and laughter;

- Read through the commitments in this book to remember the promises I have made to myself; and/or

- Spend five minutes writing in my journal all the things I look forward to experiencing and sensing at the beach.

This way, you are not letting yourself off the hook. Instead you are putting some compassionate plans in place that still take care of your body, mind and spirit.

Another example of an obstacle may be continued criticism from your sister about your clothing choices. You really love colours and have decided that part of your process of blooming is to live these colours every day. However, you know your sister is going to hate it and is likely to tease you about it. Using the Decision-Making Matrix, you can identify that her opinion is really not important to you, and you certainly can't control it. So your plan ahead for this obstacle is to just let it go—to not engage or concern yourself with her comments and to do what feels good to you.

So now it's time to take action, remember the 'if-then' plan. Use the Decision-Making Matrix as a guide to the most appropriate response to take for each one.

Potential obstacle	If this obstacle occurs, then I will...

When it All Falls Apart

'Like the lotus flower that is born out of mud, we must honour the darkest parts of ourselves and the most painful of our life's experiences, because they are what allow us to birth our most beautiful self.'
~ Debbie Ford

Despite all the very best intentions and planning for obstacles, things may come out of nowhere that may knock you off your feet. Maybe they are external events that are so unexpected they take you by surprise. Or maybe they could be many minor things, but build up to hit you hard on a day when you are too tired to deal with them constructively. When these things happen, they may be the start of a wilting process for you. Maybe not physically, but they can certainly amount to a mental, emotional or spiritual wilting.

A wilting is a situation that:

- Is highly stressful;

- Is short term—that is, it won't last a long time;

- Carries intense pressure to resolve the situation immediately; or

- A crisis.

It may seem a bit silly to define what a wilting is, but it is essential that you can identify one when it appears. The reason is it requires a significant investment in self-care. So, if you are committed to blooming, you need to be able to identify when this happens quickly and take the necessary actions. So, what do you do when everything seems to fall apart, and you don't have the energy to deal with it? What do you do when you feel mortally wounded and can't even begin to think about getting back up? Here is a five-step process to help you care for yourself during this difficult time.

1. Make a declaration. What do governments do when an unexpected and serious event occurs? They declare a state of emergency. This is more than just a political announcement. It is a way to rally the troops to take the immediate actions necessary to protect the people and prevent further disaster. This is exactly what you need to do for

yourself. It may be hard to get your head out of panic mode or your body out from underneath the blankets, but when you do have a moment of insight and it feels like you are in a middle of a crisis, then it is likely you are. Name it for what it is—a sharp and acute event that will require intervention to make it through well. There is no way you are going to be able to think logically in crisis mode. Your brain has gone into animal instinct and is prepared to fight, run away or shut down altogether. This state could last minutes or days and will require dedicated self-care to get out from.

2. Find a way to calm down. If you are in a panicked state, the first step is to get your body and mind to a more peaceful place where you have the chance to be able to think more rationally. To do this, you could:

   ◊ Remove yourself from the location. Take a 'toilet break' to get away from a toxic situation or person.

   ◊ Breathe. This is the most important piece in your first-aid kit. Do the breathing exercises provided in Chapter 15 to engage your body's own relaxation system.

   ◊ Phone a friend or professional adviser who can help you work through some calming techniques. Go to the Helpful Resources section of the book for a list of contacts that are there to help in exactly these situations.

   ◊ Watch some television or go for a walk to distract you from the short-term distress.

   ◊ Take a bath or listen to some relaxing music to soothe your body and mind.

3. Check in with your energy. Take a few moments to look inwards and take stock of your energy levels. You can do this by asking yourself

the following questions:

◊ How is my physical energy at the moment? Is it hyperactive, or is it dull or slow? Are there areas of pain or tension? What is my body telling me to do? Would rest or activity be the best remedy for my current physical state? Do I need nourishment to help me think and feel better?

◊ How are my thoughts and emotions? Am I still optimistic and positive, or have my thoughts slipped into negativity? How is my mood? Am I experiencing difficult or distressing emotions?

◊ How is my spiritual energy? Do I still have a clear sense of meaning and purpose, or am I feeling lost and uncertain?

4. Seek help. If the situation you are facing is too big for you alone, then you have the responsibility to yourself and those around you to seek out help. Some people may find this difficult as they have a view of what a strong and independent person looks like. But asking for help is not a sign of weakness. It is a show of great strength and courage and a sign of commitment to your full blooming. Yes, it takes vulnerability and humility to seek and accept help, but remember it is only courage that will get you to your *Body Beautiful*.

5. Learn. When the crisis eases, the most important thing you can do is to learn from the experience. When you are ready, reflect on the experience and ask yourself the following questions:

◊ How was I caring for myself before the crisis? Was I taking care of my body, thoughts and emotions well enough, or could my lack of self-care contributed to this crisis?

◊ What did I do well during this crisis? Where should I be congratulated for taking helpful and caring actions?

◊   Were any of my reactions to the events unhelpful? What were the triggers for these? What would I do differently next time?

◊   What resources did I use that were helpful during this crisis?

◊   What did I learn about myself from this crisis? What was the gift that this crisis has presented for my journey to blooming?

Although it may not feel like it at the time, when things fall apart, it provides the most beautiful opportunity to rebuild. This time you have the chance to rebuild on your terms and with your insights. That is, in a way that is more understanding and kind to your unique and beautiful seed.

'When our world falls apart, and we have no
more faces to wear—that's when it's beautiful,
and that's when we change.'
~ Jon Foreman

WHAT NEXT?

My greatest wish is that you can be kind, compassionate and caring towards yourself through the inevitable ups and downs that will be on your journey to blooming. There will be days when everyone is right behind you, and days when it feels like the whole world is against you. There will be days full of sun and refreshing breezes, and dark stormy days full of thunder and hail. There will be many days that fluctuate between sun and storm. But as Pema Chodron reminds us: 'You are the sky. Everything else is just the weather.' No-one or nothing can take away the true beauty that lies within you. My only hope is that in our time together I have provided you with the motivation and support to let your unique beauty shine.

So, what is next for you is your blooming. I am so excited for you and I am here cheering you on.

COMMITMENT STATEMENT

I commit to using obstacles on my path as gifts
to continue my learning and growth.
I commit to caring for myself throughout the
journey, especially on those days that feel difficult.
I commit to supporting myself to bloom.

CONCLUSION

Every flower you see around you has been through an arduous journey of growth. From a tiny seed, it battled relentlessly through the elements to give you the gift of its beauty. It did not give up despite the wind or the rain. It kept growing day by day because it had one clear mission—to bloom. The laws of nature that govern this flower also apply to us. Within each of us, there is a precious seed. It is desperate to fulfil its mission to bloom and to share its gifts with the world. But unlike a seed growing in the garden, we impose so many expectations and burdens on ourselves. We compare ourselves to a barrage of beauty standards, and then spend precious time, money and energy trying to fix ourselves to live up to them.

The result? When we are trying to make our bodies fit in, our spirit (seed) gets lost, trapped and begins pleading to be let out. Our body and seed become disconnected, and the war begins. While our seed is calling to be let free and loved, we battle with our body to look like others who tell us how it should be presented in the world. We spend our days struggling with feelings of shame, sadness and fear for the way we look, how we behave and what we believe.

What is the purpose of this war? Are you seeking acknowledgement, acceptance, adoration or love from others? What if you didn't have to fight yourself or body to get this? What if you could give all of this to yourself—be at peace with your body and live consciously and courageously with your body and seed?

This is exactly the gift that *Body Beautiful* has given you. Throughout this book, you have been shown the path to peace with your body, mind and spirit. You have been shown the path to bloom. There are two key stages to this path:

1. Consciousness. Awareness is the first step to understanding the beautiful seed within, and what has been holding you back from blooming. Throughout the first section of *Body Beautiful*, The Retreat, we have created the space and time for consciousness and to reflect on:

   ◊   The roles our bodies play in our lives;

   ◊   Societal standards of physical beauty and how they influence our thoughts, feelings and actions;

   ◊   How beauty is a matter of maturity;

   ◊   How the beliefs you have about yourself have shaped your life;

   ◊   How the past may be holding you back; and

   ◊   The perfect beauty that you hold inside.

Through The Retreat, we stopped and listened to our spirit and its calls to grow and bloom. The Retreat provided you with the opportunity to come home to your true and beautiful self, and to reconnect with your mission.

2. Courage. The second stage of the path is using the wisdom we have reconnected with to move forth and fulfil our mission to bloom. This is what The Expedition does. It places us firmly on an adventurous journey to become our fullest and most authentic self. The Expedition showed you how to move beyond past limitations and to nurture your body, mind, emotions and spirit. It helped you foresee and plan for the obstacles along the way, and care for yourself through the challenges

that arise. Specifically, The Expedition has shown you how to:

◊   Move from a place of self-esteem to self-compassion;

◊   Get confidence along the path;

◊   Investigate how your physical and social environments may be helping or hindering your journey;

◊   Care for your body as the home for your unique spirit;

◊   Care for your thoughts and feelings; and

◊   Stay connected with your spirit.

All the way throughout this book, I have asked the question, 'What Next?' The answer to this question is now up to you.

You are the designer of your own life. You have the opportunity right now to move through the lower levels of consciousness, embrace your power and create a life that is true to your seed. I wish I could tell you that the journey to bloom will be easy, but we must pass through many challenges of shame, guilt, fear, anger and pride before we can arrive at the place of joy and love. It is not a matter of if these challenges will arise; it is only a matter of how we shall face them when they do. My hope is that *Body Beautiful* has given you the insight and tools you need to understand that they exist to help you grow and, if you let them, will deliver precious gifts of growth.

My greatest wish for you is to feel freedom and joy, be at peace with your body and live a life where you love being you. Knowing when you share your unique spirit, it will radiate throughout the world, inspiring and uniting others to see the beauty within and to share their unique beauty with the world too.

In a world where we are pressured to 'fit in', I am leaving you with the challenge to 'stand out'. I dare you to see yourself clearly, accept yourself fully, love yourself deeply and teach others to do the same. Never forget that I am cheering you on in what is the greatest adventure of your life.

Your courage will be an inspiration for many generations to come.

But it all begins with you—Bloom.

WHAT NEXT?

Remembering these written words within your hands, are always here, whenever you need a loving guide. You always have the tools, resources and knowledge available to you. And because, my friend, the journey doesn't end here. If you've enjoyed this book, and you'd like to further explore how you can continue to improve and optimise every area of your life, head to www. suzzihartery.com for words of wisdom and bonus *Body Beautiful* content.

Listen to my podcast Love Being You on Apple Podcast/iTunes or Spotify, plus pop over and let's connect on Instagram @suzzihartery. Here you'll see my incredible illustrations that continue to boost your confidence, transform your imagination away from the perfect selfie and give you full permission to bloom. Plus providing you with bestie stories that are heart-filled, real and happiness boosting, with a dash to always remind you to believe that you can and will forever bloom in mind, body and spirit too.

"I look forward to hearing how your seed is flourishing on your path to blooming beautiful!"
~ Suzzi Hartery

Scan here to find out more

Helpful Resources

If you are experiencing any distressing feelings and would like someone to talk this through with, please contact the following organisation helplines that are confidential and anonymous if you require. They would love to further support you.

BEYOND BLUE

www.beyondblue.org.au

1300 22 4636 (toll-free)

Beyond Blue runs 24/7 and is a national organisation associated with depression and anxiety. All calls are one-on-one with a trained mental health professional and completely confidential.

BLACK DOG INSTITUTE

www.mycompass.org.au

The Black Dog Institute provides a 24-hour free mobile phone/computer-based program to assist those with mild to moderate depression, anxiety and stress.

THE BUTTERFLY FOUNDATION

https://butterfly.org.au

1800 33 4673

A national organisation for Australians impacted by eating disorders and body image issues. Providing support via email, webchat or phone from 8am to midnight AEST 7 days a week.

KIDS HELP LINE

www.kidshelp.com.au

1800 55 1800

Kids Help Line is a free and confidential telephone counselling service for five to twenty-five-year-olds in Australia. Available support 24/07 via email, webchat or phone.

LIFELINE AUSTRALIA

www.lifeline.org.au

13 11 14

Lifeline Australia provides 27/7 telephone counselling service for adults needing emotional support. They even have a text service.

MENSLINE AUSTRALIA

https://mensline.org.au

1300 789 978

MensLine Australia offers 24/7 telephone and online counselling support for men with concerns about mental health, anger management, family violence (using and experiencing), addiction, relationship, stress and wellbeing.

QLife

https://qlife.org.au

1800 184 527

QLife provides anonymous, LGBTI peer support and referral for people wanting to talk about a range of issues including sexuality, identity, gender, bodies, feelings or relationships. Available daily 3pm to midnight for telephone or webchat support.

Appendix 1 – Descriptive Words

Helpful Self-Descriptions

Active	Cultured	Forgiving	Liberal
Adaptable	Curious	Forthright	Logical
Adventurous	Daring	Freethinking	Lovable
Appreciative	Decisive	Friendly	Loyal
Articulate	Dedicated	Fun-loving	Magnanimous
Aspiring	Deep	Generous	Many-sided
Athletic	Dignified	Gentle	Mature
Attractive	Disciplined	Genuine	Methodical
Balanced	Discreet	Good-natured	Meticulous
Benevolent	Dramatic	Gracious	Moderate
Brilliant	Dutiful	Hardworking	Modest
Calm	Dynamic	Healthy	Neat
Capable	Earnest	Helpful	Objective
Caring	Educated	Heroic	Observant
Charismatic	Efficient	Honest	Open
Charming	Elegant	Honourable	Optimistic
Cheerful	Eloquent	Humble	Organised
Clear-headed	Empathetic	Humorous	Original
Clever	Energetic	Idealistic	Passionate
Colourful	Enthusiastic	Imaginative	Patient
Compassionate	Exciting	Incorruptible	Peaceful
Conciliatory	Extraordinary	Independent	Perceptive
Confident	Fair	Individualistic	Perfectionistic
Conscientious	Faithful	Innovative	Persuasive
Considerate	Farsighted	Insightful	Playful
Contemplative	Firm	Intelligent	Practical
Cooperative	Fit	Intuitive	Pretty
Courageous	Flexible	Kind	Principled
Courteous	Focused	Knowledge	Profound
Creative	Forceful	Leader-oriented	Protective

Prudent	Selfless	Strong	Uncomplaining
Punctual	Self-reliant	Studious	Understanding
Purposeful	Self-sufficient	Suave	Venturesome
Rational	Sensitive	Subtle	Vivacious
Realistic	Sentimental	Sweet	Warm
Reflective	Sexy	Sympathetic	Well-read
Relaxed	Simple	Systematic	Well-rounded
Reliable	Skilful	Tasteful	Wise
Resourceful	Sophisticated	Teacher-oriented	Witty
Respectful	Spontaneous	Thorough	Worthy
Responsible	Sporting	Tidy	
Romantic	Stable	Tolerant	
Sane	Steady	Tractable	
Scholarly	Stoic	Trusting	

Problematic Self-Descriptions

Aggressive	Calculating	Crass	Disconcerting
Aimless	Callous	Crazy	Discontented
Aloof	Careless	Critical	Discouraging
Amoral	Childish	Crude	Discourteous
Angry	Clumsy	Cruel	Dishonest
Anxious	Coarse	Cynical	Disloyal
Apathetic	Cold	Decadent	Disobedient
Argumentative	Colourless	Deceitful	Disorganised
Arrogant	Complaining	Delicate	Disputatious
Artificial	Compulsive	Demanding	Disrespectful
Awkward	Conceited	Dependent	Disruptive
Bland	Conformist	Desperate	Distractible
Blunt	Contemptible	Destructive	Disturbing
Boisterous	Conventional	Devious	Domineering
Brutal	Cowardly	Difficult	Dull

Egocentric	Impractical	Negative	Rigid
Envious	Imprudent	Neurotic	Ritualistic
Erratic	Impulsive	Obese	Sadistic
Escapist	Inconsiderate	Obnoxious	Sanctimonious
Extravagant	Indecisive	Obsessive	Scheming
Extreme	Indulgent	Old	Scornful
False	Inert	Opinionated	Secretive
Fanatical	Inhibited	Opportunistic	Sedentary
Fanciful	Insecure	Oppressed	Selfish
Fat	Insensitive	Outrageous	Self-indulgent
Fatalistic	Insincere	Paranoid	Shallow
Fearful	Insulting	Passive	Short-sighted
Fickle	Intolerant	Pedantic	Sloppy
Fiery	Irrational	Petty	Slow
Fixed	Irresponsible	Plump	Sly
Flamboyant	Irritable	Pompous	Small-thinking
Forgetful	Lazy	Possessive	Stiff
Foolish	Lanky	Power-hungry	Stupid
Fraudulent	Malicious	Prejudiced	Submissive
Frightening	Mannerless	Presumptuous	Superficial
Frivolous	Meddlesome	Pretentious	Superstitious
Gloomy	Melancholic	Prim	Suspicious
Greedy	Messy	Procrastinating	Tactless
Grim	Miserable	Provocative	Tasteless
Gullible	Miserly	Puritanical	Tense
Hateful	Misguided	Quirky	Thoughtless
Haughty	Mistaken	Reactionary	Timid
Hedonistic	Money-minded	Reactive	Treacherous
Hesitant	Moody	Regimental	Trendy
Hidebound	Morbid	Regretful	Troublesome
High-handed	Naïve	Repentant	Ugly
Hostile	Narcissistic	Repressed	Unappreciative
Ignorant	Narrow	Resentful	Unattractive
Impatient	Narrow-minded	Ridiculous	Uncaring

Uncharitable	Ungrateful	Unrealistic	Vague
Unconvincing	Unhealthy	Unreflective	Venomous
Uncooperative	Unimaginative	Unreliable	Vindictive
Uncreative	Unimpressive	Unrestrained	Vulnerable
Uncritical	Unlovable	Unstable	Weak
Undisciplined	Unpolished	Unworthy	Wilful
Unfriendly	Unprincipled	Vacuous	

Appendix 2 – Emotions

Empowering Feelings and Emotions

Ambitious	Content	Inspired	Renewed
Amused	Creative	Invigorated	Secure
Appreciated	Delighted	Joyful	Strengthened
Assured	Determined	Loving	Strong
Assured	Dynamic	Marvellous	Successful
Blessed	Empowered	Motivated	Sure
Bold	Encouraged	Optimistic	Tenacious
Brave	Enthusiastic	Peaceful	Understood
Certain	Focused	Pleased	Unique
Charmed	Glad	Powerful	Vibrant
Cherished	Grateful	Prepared	Valuable
Comforted	Hardy	Refreshed	
Confident	Healthy	Relaxed	

Distressing Feelings and Emotions

Agitated	Depressed	Frozen	Isolated
Annoyed	Desperate	Frustrated	Jealous
Anxious	Disgusted	Furious	Listless
Ashamed	Dismayed	Guilty	Livid
Bitter	Doubtful	Heavy	Let down
Bored	Drained	Hesitant	Lonely
Burned out	Dull	Hurt	Lost
Confused	Embarrassed	Impaired	Mad
Critical	Exhausted	Indecisive	Mixed up
Crushed	Fatigued	Indifferent	Mournful
Damaged	Fed up	Inferior	Outraged
Dejected	Forgotten	Irritated	Pathetic

Perplexed	Resentful	Stunned	Upset
Pessimistic	Self-conscious	Tender	Weary
Powerless	Shocked	Tense	Weepy
Punished	Shy	Troubled	Wounded
Raging	Sorrowful	Uncertain	
Rejected	Stale	Uncomfortable	
Repugnant	Stuck	Unsure	

Appendix 3 – List of Values

Authenticity	Curiosity	Kindness	Religion
Achievement	Determination	Knowledge	Reputation
Adventure	Fairness	Leadership	Respect
Autonomy	Faith	Learning	Responsibility
Balance	Fame	Love	Security
Beauty	Friendships	Loyalty	Self-respect
Boldness	Fun	Meaningful work	Service
Compassion	Growth	Openness	Spirituality
Challenge	Happiness	Optimism	Stability
Citizenship	Honesty	Peace	Success
Community	Humour	Pleasure	Status
Competency	Influence	Poise	Trustworthiness
Contribution	Inner harmony	Popularity	Wealth
Creativity	Justice	Recognition	Wisdom

References

1   Becker, A., Burwell, R., Gilman, S., Herzog, D., & Hamburg, P. (2002). Eating behaviours and attitudes following prolonged exposure to television among ethnic Fijian adolescent girls. *The British journal of psychiatry : the journal of mental science, 180*, 509-14 .

2   Martin, J.B. (2010). The Development of Ideal Body Image Perceptions in the United States. *Nutrition Today, 45*, 98-110.

3   Blackstock, C. (2011, October 23). The ugly side of heroin chic. Retrieved from https://www.independent.co.uk/news/the-ugly-side-of-heroin-chic-1235403.html [Accessed 17 August 2020].

4   National Eating Disorders Association. 2020. *Statistics & Research On Eating Disorders.* [online] Available at: https://www.nationaleatingdisorders. org/statistics-research-eating-disorders [Accessed 17 August 2020].

5   Hawkins, David R. *Power Vs. Force: The Hidden Determinants of Human Behavior.* Carlsbad: Hay House, 2014.

6   "What Self-Awareness Really Is (and How to Cultivate It)." *Harvard Business Review.* Last modified January 4, 2018. https://hbr.org/2018/01/what-self-awareness-really-is-and-how-to-cultivate-it. [Accessed 7 September 2020].

7   Gilovich, T., Medvec, V. H., & Savitsky, K. (2000). *The spotlight effect in social judgment: An egocentric bias in estimates of the salience of one's own actions and appearance.* Journal of Personality and Social Psychology, 78(2), 211–222.

8   Gilovich, T., Kruger, J., & Medvec, V. H. (2002). *The spotlight effect revisited: overestimating manifest variability of our actions and appearance.* Journal of Experimental Social Psychology, 38, 93-99. Retrieved April 11, 2017

9   Moss, Michael. *Salt, Sugar, Fat: How the Food Giants Hooked Us.* New York: Random House, 2013.

10   Cdc.gov. 2020. [online] Available at: https://www.cdc.gov/Diabetes/statistics/slides/long_term_trends.pdf [Accessed 15 August 2020].

11   Krueger, J., Vohs, K. and Baumeister, R., 2008. Is the allure of self-esteem a mirage after all? *American Psychologist*, 63(1), pp.64-65.

12   Harris, Russ, and Steven Hayes. *The Confidence Gap: A Guide to Overcoming Fear and Self-doubt*. Boulder: Shambhala Publications, 2011.

13   Ibid.

14   Strauss, Clara, Billie Lever Taylor, Jenny Gu, Willem Kuyken, Ruth Baer, Fergal Jones, and Kate Cavanagh. "What is compassion and how can we measure it? A review of definitions and measures." *Clinical Psychology Review* 47 (2016), 15-27.

15   Massachusetts General Hospital. "'Traffic light' food labels reduce calories purchased in hospital cafeteria." ScienceDaily. ScienceDaily, 10 July 2019.

16   Healthpsych.psy.vanderbilt.edu. 2020. *Psychology Department*. [online] Available at: http://healthpsych.psy.vanderbilt.edu/color_therapy.htm [Accessed 15 August 2020].

17   Figueiro, M., Steverson, B., Heerwagen, J., Kampschroer, K., Hunter, C., Gonzales, K., Plitnick, B. and Rea, M., 2017. The impact of daytime light exposures on sleep and mood in office workers. *Sleep Health*, 3(3), pp.204-215.

18   Rawlings, R., 1999. *Healing Gardens*. London: Seven Dials.

19   Mind.org.uk. 2020. Go Green To Beat The Blues. [online] Available at: https://www.mind.org.uk/news-campaigns/news/go-green-to-beat-the-blues/. [Accessed 15 August 2020].

20   Kim, G., Jeong, G., Kim, T., Baek, H., Oh, S., Kang, H., Lee, S., Kim, Y. and Song, J., 2010. Functional Neuroanatomy Associated with Natural and Urban Scenic Views in the Human Brain: 3.0T Functional MR Imaging. Korean Journal of Radiology, 11(5), p.507.

21   Lohr, V., 2010. What are the benefits of plants indoors and why do we respond positively to them?. *Acta Horticulturae*, (881), pp.675-682.

22   Conferences.com.au. 2020. [online] Available at: http://www.conferences.com.au/wp-content/uploads/2018/04/1130-Joelle.pdf [Accessed 16 August 2020].

23   The Conversation. 2020. *Women Can Build Positive Body Image By Controlling What They View On Social Media*. [online] Available at: https://theconversation.com/women-can-build-positive-body-image-by-controlling-what-they-view-on-social-media-113041 [Accessed 16 August 2020].

24   Fardouly, J. and Vartanian, L., 2015. Negative comparisons about one's appearance mediate the relationship between Facebook usage and body image concerns. *Body Image*, 12, pp.82-88.

25   Fowler, J. and Christakis, N., 2008. Dynamic spread of happiness in a large social network: longitudinal analysis over 20 years in the Framingham Heart Study. *BMJ*, 337(dec04 2), pp.a2338-a2338.

26   Giles, L., 2005. Effect of social networks on 10 year survival in very old Australians: the Australian longitudinal study of aging. *Journal of Epidemiology & Community Health*, 59(7), pp.574-579.

27   Huffingtonpost.com.au. 2020. Available at: https://www.huffingtonpost.com.au/entry/qualities-of-real-friends_n_5709821 [Accessed 16 August 2020].

28   Makin, S., 2020. *Deep Sleep Gives Your Brain A Deep Clean*. [online] Scientific American. Available at: https://www.scientificamerican.com/article/deep-sleep-gives-your-brain-a-deep-clean1/ [Accessed 20 August 2020].

29   Pal, G.K. Velkumary, S. and Madanmohan. (2004). *Effect of short-term practice of breathing exercises on autonomic functions in normal human volunteers*. Indian Journal of Medical Research, 120, 115-121.

30   Caroline Leaf, *Who Switched Off My Brain?* (Dallas: Improv, Ltd. 2008), 14.

31   Adapted from Notice, Name and Neutralise developed by Dr Russ Harris and published in the following book: Harris, R., 2008. *The Happiness Trap*. Shambala Press.

32   Hockenbury, D. and Hockenbury, S.E. (2007). *Discovering Psychology*. New York: Worth Publishers.

33   Dethmer, J., Chapman, D. and Klemp, K., n.d. *The 15 Commitments Of Conscious Leadership*.

34   Taylor, J. B. (2006). *My stroke of insight: A brain scientist's personal journey*. New York, NY: Penguin Books.

35   Jack, R., Garrod, O. and Schyns, P., 2014. Dynamic Facial Expressions of Emotion Transmit an Evolving Hierarchy of Signals over Time. *Current Biology*, 24(2), pp.187-192.

36   Nummenm, L., Glereana, E., Harib, R. and K. Hietanend, J.,
2020. *Bodily Map Of Emotions*. [online] Pnas.org. Available at: https://www.
pnas.org/content/pnas/early/2013/12/26/1321664111.full.pdf [Accessed 24
August 2020].

37   Nytimes.com. 2020. *Olympians Use Imagery As Mental Training*. [online]
Available at: https://www.nytimes.com/2014/02/23/sports/olympics/
olympians-use-imagery-as-mental-training.html [Accessed 2 September
2020].

38   Psychology Today. 2020. Seeing Is Believing: The Power Of
Visualization. [online] Available at: https://www.psychologytoday.com/gb/
blog/flourish/200912/seeing-is-believing-the-power-visualization [Accessed 2
September 2020].

39   Sidsavara.com. 2020. *Written Commitment Research Summary*.
[online] Available at: https://sidsavara.com/wp-content/uploads/2008/09/
researchsummary2.pdf [Accessed 21 August 2020].

40   The concept was originally created by Paul J. Meyer, founder of Success
Motivation® Institute, Inc.

you for moments shared, for your support and memories. You've all reminded me (and part of the purpose of this book) that we must always stay receptive to love for all. I appreciate you all for helping me see my sunshine. Specifically mentioning those forever in my heart: Leisa Wadsworth, my sister from another mother. Kylie Ryan, my mindset shifter who got me out of a very deep rest. Grace Anderson, who showed me unconditional love. Temma Bell, my deep no filters conversationalist and cheerleader. Sarah Rock, my soul sister who allows me to fully show up as I am and gives the best insights and makes the yummiest gummies. Lee Leibrandt, your constant check-in especially through my tough times and how a zoom catch-up feels like we only spoke yesterday. Jade Burrie, for being as excited as me about being a published author and for always cheering me on— look, she is here!! Belinda Tobin, I will be forever thankful to you, as the first person I told about my book, your mentoring, support and input is valued beyond the seed we both have within us—we did it—from my whole blooming heart thank you all!

To my primary school bully. Thank you for the teachings I've been able to utilise from your days, weeks, months and years of torment making me think I wasn't good enough and never knowing why you tried to use your power on me. Without those horrific and scary moments like overgrown weeds, I wouldn't be where I am today. I wish you nothing but good health and a good state of mind. I am so thankful to be positively impacting so many lives and making a contribution to the world.

To my guides and angels, my fellow self-help and personal development leaders. Thank you for your guidance and for being lighthouses too. Our voice and messages are needed in the world. May we always shine bright and bloom proudly, so we can continue to always give everyone permission to do the same too.

Saving two of my best petals till last, an eternal thank you goes out to my fur babies. Mr Ayers and Miss Bella Rocket for being my constant, cuddle pals, loving, squishy-faced companions. You were always there at my feet on late nights, or early before sunrise mornings, you allowed for delayed play days to take place in the creation of this masterpiece. I love you both so much. I got so lucky to be your fur mum. Thank you for choosing me.

And, of course, to you my beloved reader. For having the courage, willingness, and heart to explore new insights as you evolve and return to love. It's been an honour to hold space and guide you in returning to your seed. My forever wish to you is that you continue to bloom, retreat or explore today and every day forward.

ABOUT THE AUTHOR

Shift years of deep-rooted beliefs, feel lighter and happier in your body, and return to love for yourself and all others always.

Suzzi Hartery

Suzzi Hartery, known as the Self-Worth Whisperer (crowned by her incredible community) has a soul purpose to support you to wake up every day knowing you love being you. Through her inspiring and kind-hearted voice, making spiritual and personal development content relatable, digestible, and actionable for all.

Suzzi provides a safe haven of strategies, resources and personal knowledge to guide you to reclaim your confidence, reignite your self-compassion, evolve your self-esteem and up-level your mindset so you can achieve your aligned dreams.

Aside from the authentic life experience, knowing Suzzi only shares what she has experienced, learned or is going through. With many qualifications that came from posing one question she always used to ask: 'What am I here to do?'. This led to following her instincts in getting qualified in NLP, hypnotherapy, health coaching, life coaching and two bachelor degrees of which her most recent is in Health Science specialising in Naturopathy.

Suzzi knows that you can take what you need to inspire you and wants you to know she is here as your cheerleader—part of your support team, just like she knows you are for her.

'It's time to return home to yourself—your true self—love.
Thank you for joining me and thank you for being you.'
~ Love Suzzi x